The Art of Feeling Good

The Art of
Feeling Good

The Power of Àse Yoga

Dr. Robbin Alston

iUniverse, Inc.
Bloomington

The Art of Feeling Good
The Power of Àse Yoga

iUniverse books may be ordered through booksellers or by contacting:

iUniverse
1663 Liberty Drive
Bloomington, IN 47403
www.iuniverse.com
1-800-Authors (1-800-288-4677)

Because of the dynamic nature of the Internet, any web addresses or links
contained in this book may have changed since publication and may no
longer be valid. The views expressed in this work are solely those of the
author and do not necessarily reflect the views of the publisher, and the
publisher hereby disclaims any responsibility for them.

Any people depicted in stock imagery provided by Thinkstock are
models, and such images are being used for illustrative purposes only.

Certain stock imagery © Thinkstock.

ISBN: 978-1-4759-5877-5 (sc)
ISBN: 978-1-4759-6295-6 (hc)
ISBN: 978-1-4759-5879-9 (e)

Library of Congress Control Number: 2012921562

Printed in the United States of America

iUniverse rev. date: 12/5/2012

For my mother, Dorothea Barnes,
who revealed to me the unlimited power
of the unseen.

Contents

Acknowledgments .1

My Initiation .3

Author's Reflection 5

The Awakening 13

The Simple Truth 21

The Unveiling 25

Who Is Practicing Yoga? 31

If Not Yoga, Then What? 33

Who Are We? 39

What Is Going On? 43

Embracing Right Knowledge 53

Personal Responsibility 63

The Power of Aset, an African Deity 65

The Balancing Power of Àse Yoga 71

The Breaths of Liberation 83

Breath Connection 85

Meditation 91

Feeling Good: Chakra Tuning. 95

Our Seven Major Energy Centers 99

The Greatest Love of All Resides Inside You 107

You've Got the Power. 113

It's Time for Love, So Let's Get Ready. 117

Express Yourself. 121

The Power of Knowing 125

Beautiful Woman: Feel Good 129

Appendix A 133

Appendix B 137

Bibliography. 139

Acknowledgments

thank all of the women who inspired me to write this book. Some I know; many I do not know, but I feel their spirits. I also express my deepest gratitude to the countless women who took time to complete the Àse (ah-shay) yoga surveys. I grasped what you said and didn't say about your lives.

I extend heartfelt gratitude to Rita Hart, my sister, for her support and insight into our rarely discussed yet dangerous liaison with the healthcare system which includes rescheduling our medical appointments, not prioritizing our health and waiting too long to seek treatment. Statistics and Center-for-Disease-Control reports aside, our ability to feel good lies in relearning how to take care of our bodies, minds, and spirits. I am especially grateful to Ron Allen and Malcolm Alston for the manifestation of their Àse within the beautiful photography.

I give eternal gratitude to the few but courageous warrior spirits, authors, scholars, and practitioners who have expended their precious life force to unearth valuable knowledge and treasures that boldly reveal the values of our progenitors of yoga, our ancient ancestors in Kemet. I thank Dr. Asa Hilliard for his work connects us to yoga by realigning our minds to truth by encouraging the liberation and defragmentation of our minds. Often, we describe the struggles of our ancestors as the activities of activists rather than that of spiritual healers, shamans, gurus, or yogis. Yet our ancestors' words transmit an eternal message that encourages us to unlock our life force and open our spiritual energies.

I say to the millions of heroic but often forgotten beautiful African heroines—our foremothers and ancestors who were brutally captured and harmed—to the warrior queens who struggled, fought, resisted, and died for our freedom; to the forgotten goddesses, and to the wise women I have met that I stand on your shoulders, forever indebted. I am because you are.

Your experiences must be remembered, respected, and understood because they hold the key to our healing. We must neither forget you nor be ashamed. We must begin to feel the love, the energy, and the power that will ultimately heal us.

With awe-inspiring gratitude and appreciation, I thank the omniscient divine soul Ba, God, my ancestors, my *Ka* for the manifestation of Àse yoga. When we connect with this indomitable energy, life holds infinite possibilities and we feel good.

What will motivate us to be better than we are? What will inspire us to do instead of dream, to become instead of simply exist? What has to happen for us to wake up? An accident, an illness, discontent, a loss, famine, or simply hitting rock bottom?

When will we realize that the choices we make affect not only us but also our children? Our choices have consequences, and we reap what we sow. We can't make unwise choices and expects positive results. When we act on impulse rather than insight, we suffer. Wake up. Only then will your lives become what they should be, instead of what they are.

My Initiation

An initiation is a formal process that helps you grow, mature, and acquire knowledge. That knowledge is converted into wisdom, which improves the community. In Western society, we are initiated into sororities and secret societies, religious affiliations, social groups, and education and certificate programs that all too often focused on the individual. However, in indigenous societies, walimus (teachers), the shaman, swami, priest, and priestess were initiated for the betterment of the community. In the West, we give ourselves titles of respect; in ancient societies, people were given designations in accordance with their divine purposes.

In our innate quest to belong and be more than who we are, we are initiated into groups with the mind-set of exclusivity rather than of service or transformation. Our modern-day initiations are replete with egotism rather than divine callings.

Life, however, has an initiation process that sometimes takes you to someone like a guru and at other times guides you on a nonphysical level to spiritual teachers. You cannot purchase this type of initiation; it is acquired through direct experiences. These experiences contain a message that tells you what to do next. It is then that you realize your previous experiences were a preparation and a lesson for a higher purpose.

When I think about my life, this initiation process makes sense. I've climbed mountains, slain the wild beast, swam through dangerous waters, survived off the land, and fought to stay alive. My upbringing reflects the oppression of the times. Through my initiation rites and from conception through birth, I was ushered into chaos and confusion that could have destroyed me. Instead, these experiences served as the basis for my awakening during which infinite possibilities were unveiled. One of those possibilities guided me to use my breath as antidote against everything I had encountered and would encounter.

As I practiced connecting to my breath, I discovered who I was meant to be, not who I was becoming as a result of my experiences. Breath is the path to transformation. When I embarked on my breathing journey, my vital energy centers opened and Àse yoga was born.

Author's Reflection

"We the women will.
—Yaa Astawaa

As a psychologist, breast cancer survivor, and yogini, I felt compelled to write *The Art of Feeling Good*. With each passing moment, I felt a responsibility to take action and be candid. I was filled with a sense of urgency. This book became a *personal responsibility* on my part to those who paved the way for me. *The Art of Feeling Good* is an invitation for women who are the descendants of extraordinary historical trauma to reclaim their inheritance of peace. With peace, we are balanced, healthy, and fulfilled. But how do we get there? By being in harmony with our true selves.

As we all know, many obstacles stand in the way of attaining peace. Certainly, some of those obstacles are within us. However, I've come to realize that other obstacles are historically ingrained. Through the centuries, something happened to African-American women that created an energetic imbalance on the deepest level. One often-overlooked experience is the penetrating psycho-spiritual impact of the enslavement process on African-American women. As I listened to women share stories about their childhoods, early experiences, relationships, mothers, and grandmothers, it became obvious that they were hiding something deep within what some call the unconscious. Whether discussing their work, relationships, and or home lives, many of these women seemed to be reacting to situations that were implanted eons ago. Our mothers, and their mothers too often inadvertently deposited within us their enslavement and post-enslavement pain and suffering.

Too many women settle for the hand they've been dealt, foregoing any possibility of peace. Without peace, we have chaos, which causes us to live in a state of imbalance. That imbalance can lead to disease, illness, toxic relationships, and harmful choices. I maintain that the ideology, worldview, and experiences during and perhaps even before the transatlantic slave trade left an enduring wound in African-American women. The thought process that fostered slavery created an internal conflict in many African-American women, whose sense of stability, nurturance, self-image, self-worth, and feelings of intimacy, empowerment, and truth became distorted. This distortion struck deeply into our vital energy centers, affecting our physical, emotional, and spiritual wellbeing.

While it may be uncomfortable to bring up slavery, it must be discussed. That dehumanizing experience—during which horrific physical, psychological, and social tortures occurred—created an energetic disequilibrium and disturbance within the body's energy field that influenced the way people think, feel, and act. Have you ever wondered why you feel abandoned when a relationship ends, or why you hold onto toxic relationships? Why do some of us dislike our physical appearances? Why do we alter our images to look like someone else? It may have more to do with our historical conditioning than our current situations. It may have to do with a mind-set of enslavement rather than one of emancipation. Several factors—political, social, and psychological—may be feeding our internal battles with ourselves, and our only recourse is a personalized, self-healing process.

How do we heal? For me, the answer is clear: yoga. Why? Yoga is transformative and supports our journey toward peace. By helping us become conscious and aware, yoga ramps up our energy so we can let go of thoughts, actions, and deeds that impede our peace of mind. With yoga, we connect to right knowledge, which is a natural branch of our healing journey.

Why Àse yoga? Àse yoga explores our individual journeys and the stories that influence us today. In doing so, it acknowledges the uniqueness of our being and experiences. Moreover, it activates the innate power for self-healing within all beings.

When you practice Àse yoga, you receive the gift, i.e., the ability to feel real love, inner health, and wholeness. With Àse yoga, you grow through individual and personal relationships. It doesn't matter how long ago the trauma occurred; the lack of healing sustains our false sense of self and damages us. Accompanying the trauma are thoughts that become our reality. Nothing happens to us that doesn't have consequences. As with any trauma, this enduring experience—slavery—gradually began to define us. Consider this: Is it so farfetched to believe that our foremothers—who endured forced displacement, enslavement, image distortion, the Great Depression, and the Jim Crow laws—would have transmitted their fears, stress, helplessness, anger, depression, disappointment, confusion, and imbalances to us? No, it is not.

That's why Àse yoga activates our powerful capacity for self-healing by converting previous unbalanced experiences into dynamic lessons of transformation. In Àse yoga, we unravel suppressed experiences with a practice that provides the atmosphere for releasing pain and accepting personal responsibility. In the process, we become receptive to ancestral wisdom, which reveals to us how to be at peace with the present moment. This practice is based on the belief that we can't live in the here-and-now until we explore the past. Over the years, we've been conditioned to ignore, misunderstand, disassociate, and, yes, forget ourselves. We hold in our feelings, not realizing that suppression is not a form of healing and our early experiences do matter.

It took time and personal upheaval for me to realize that being at peace was long overdue and fraught with obstacles. To understand the obstacles in my path, however, I had to connect with my deceased mother. A journey into her life revealed that she was unstable, insecure, and unhappy. Because I was part of her, I went through life feeling uncertain, unstable, and not grounded. How could she give me hope? How could she give me a sense of grounding, self-worth, or inner power? How could she give me something she did not have?

Consider my experience and reflect on your own life with your mother, aunts, grandmothers, and sisters. Our childhood interactions with our caretakers become the way we respond to the world and ourselves as adults.

In my case, obstacle after obstacle kept coming into my life. I grew weary along my journey. Eventually, I was shown insights that lifted me up and opened my eyes. I stopped focusing on what my mother didn't give me and instead concentrated on what she had given me: an opportunity to heal. My presence and my experiences had meaning. Peace came when I found meaning in my life. Initially, I'd seen the backlash from slavery and my personal challenges as obstacles to peace. After deeper reflection, I realized that we sustain our oppressive experiences through our thoughts and lifestyles.

Thoughts are powerful transmitters of the positive and the negative. How we perceive our life experiences determines our focus. Say you grew up thinking all men will be unfaithful. Perhaps your father was unfaithful to your mother. If so, you might be preoccupied with not getting hurt, and you might be guarded and mistrustful in your relationships. You meet many nice men, but you think they're all like your father. Love is secondary to protecting your ego and heart. You walk around looking angry and feeling defensive. The way you think about your situation or life experiences becomes the driving force in your daily activities. For me, changing my life coincided with changing my thoughts. Although it didn't change what had happened to me previously, it did change my subsequent experiences.

Unfortunately, such changes are not easy because it is hard to let go of our attachment to the way we think. Nevertheless, this attachment also blocks our blessings. In addition, it is difficult for us to rise above our current situation or what someone has done to us and see the immense opportunity for healing. We may refuse to budge or let go of our anger even if that is what's best for us. *As a result, our thoughts either nourish our liberation or sustain our enslavement.* Clearly, enslavement behavior will exist as long as our thoughts fail to transcend our experience and our lifestyles fail to support healthiness. It is not enough to talk about what happened, either historically or personally; we must do something to create balance and exact wholeness.

Àse yoga is an empowering healing practice that attends to our thought processes, which encapsulate our energy centers. It restores and reconnects us to our authentic spiritual identity. We've forgotten our real identities. We see ourselves in comparison to others, while our real identities stay buried and forgotten in the depths of our unconscious. As long as we dismiss who we are and hold on to the belief that "it doesn't matter nowadays," we will remain in a state of chaos.

This practice, an energetic restitution process encourages us to understand past feelings, confusion, distress, or humiliations; restore our self-worth and health; and fulfill our purpose. To accomplish these goals, we must begin to contextualize the past and prioritize the wisdom and beauty we possess. What happens to us in life must not be the sum of who we become. Who we become must be connected to truth. Otherwise, we cannot have honest relationships with others. We become a byproduct of someone else's creation; we become an extension of suffering. Only through healing can we embrace an authentic sense of self, fulfill our purpose, and rediscover the art of feeling good.

I wrote this book to enlighten and inspire all people everywhere to practice self-care, self-love, and self-healing through self-knowledge. It is written through the lens of my experience because a lot can be learned from the experiences of others. Some have told me that in focusing on the experiences of African-American women, I have limited and perhaps narrowed my narrative. Some felt that it would be better to generalize the book, particularly if I wanted others to buy it. I realize how easy it is to compromise and not follow your heart because of what others say. How many of us have deferred our dreams? However, I decided against their suggestions and remained true to myself. I wanted to write a book that reflected my worldview. *The Art of Feeling Good* is about following my heart.

The unpleasant truth is that according to the Agency for Healthcare Research and Quality, the National Center on Health Statistics, the Center for Disease Control, and the African-American women and Black Women's Health Project, African-American women are dying too young, succumbing to preventable diseases, and experiencing disproportionately high incidences of high blood pressure, cancer, and strokes. We have issues that go unanswered, unaddressed, and unresolved. To pretend that everything is all right and diminish the seriousness of our struggles only leads to chronic suffering and self-defeating behavior. In the end, only through a healing practice can we counteract the effects of our personal and historical traumas.

Within these pages, as I share my personal awakening after near-death experiences, creative energy flows forth as words from my heart to yours. .

As we continue this journey, we dispel the myth that defines yoga as a movement or an exercise. In this book, we explore who is practicing yoga and what is going on in our lives. When we stand back, it is evident that healing is necessary regardless of social class, occupation, or education. We owe ourselves the privilege of healing.

Healing opens portals of closed energy. Thoughts are energy, and energy is life. This book is a manifestation of the energy Àse that is more than a response to a call. It is an active power that longs to be awakened. We all possess this powerful energy.

The Art of Feeling Good awakens you. It encourages you to let your light shine, manifest your amazing self, and fulfill your purpose. It will take you on a journey into listening, meditation, reflection, breath awareness, cosmic rhythms, and poses known as asanas. As we release energy from our tailbones to the crown of our heads, we will worry less about our basic needs and no longer question our beauty or self-worth. As we grow, we will let go of negative thoughts and no longer have issues with communication or love. We will forgive others and ourselves. We will speak from the heart. We will listen with our hearts.

Our minds will become less restless and less agitated. We will let go of disappointments and heartaches. We will let go of low self-esteem, which is a barrier to our creativity or sexuality. We will feel stable, grounded, and secure. Life will be different because we will have connected to our divinity, our breath, and our inner goddesses. Something extraordinary will happen. We will release negative situations and circumstances into the bosom of Mother Earth. Healing will emerge. We will begin to smile, let down our guards, lift our heads, and open up our hearts.

With the power of Àse yoga, we embrace that greatness that lies within us. When we do, we reveal our natural beauty, unique gifts and talents, and glorious truth, which transforms our lives. In this precious moment, open yourself to feel the energy of the African goddess Aset—the giver of life, the remover of obstacles. Salute your divine light within. Boldly share positive feelings as you blossom through *The Art of Feeling Good.*

Àse, Àse.

The Awakening

*The African Universe has an inherent life-force which
we may conceive as underlying energy inherent in
everything and of which the Supreme Being is the source.*
—Chukwunyere Kamulu

After I was diagnosed with breast cancer in 1998, an intense feeling came over me. It was clear that I wanted to heal. I set out to delve deeper into my life to understand the insecurities, unstable background, emotional challenges, and environmental factors that had led up to a radical mastectomy of the left breast. I asked myself, *Where did four four-millimeter cancer cells come from? How did I get here?*

Through extensive meditation and inner reflection the answer was clear: I was clinging to the past, and the past was clinging on to me. I wanted to live, so I set out to thoroughly change how I had been living. I did the unthinkable. I quit my job, focused on being healthy, and completed my studies in psychology.

Cancer scared me into fighting to live. Suddenly cul-de-sac relationships, sexiness, unfulfilling work, and "sweating the small stuff" no longer seemed important. Any anger I harbored also slipped away. I began to ask myself: *Who am I? Where am I right now? What am I supposed to do with my life?* However, I was unable to answer these questions.

I meditated on healing my body. What was revealed to me is that the body heals along with the mind and the spirit. Doctors can cut off a part of your body, but the ability to heal lies within your own hands. Although cancer is a physical manifestation of dis-ease and imbalances, it ousted years of confused thinking. It also brought my harmful, unconscious thoughts and behaviors to the surface.

Over the years, I'd grown accustomed to thinking a certain way. This thinking was likely a reaction to my upbringing. Seeds of low self-esteem, mis-education, inferiority, insecurity, and impoverishment had taken root and grown into a tangled web of faulty thinking. As cancer cells invaded my body, this thinking obstructed my healing. I had adopted thoughts about the world and myself that were not healthy or true. I realized that the same way I learned unhealthy behaviors I could learn healthy behaviors. To do so, I entered a period of deep introspection, which led to me to yoga.

Intimidation set in the moment I entered the first yoga studio. I saw a flexible, white female going through motions I had never seen before. Interestingly, but not surprisingly, she didn't seem to see me. I felt invisible. As she moved through the postures, or asanas, with finesse and chilliness, I decided not return. Isn't that how we typically respond when we face something uncomfortable? We usually give up. Yet often the very obstacle that we run away from is, indeed, the one we need to master. In this case, a rather persistent inner voice urged me to return.

I returned to yoga, but this time, I detached myself from the instructor. Gradually, I stopped seeing the teacher's personality and started focusing on my own *Journey of Ra* (also known as the sun salutation). The teacher's technical skills were masterful. I absorbed the skills and left the rest. It didn't matter whether she liked me or not. Once I detached from her disposition, she seemed to smile more and announced a new teacher would take her place. However, her presence no longer mattered. I needed to learn less about the asanas and more about listening to my inner voice.

They say that when a student is ready, the right teacher will appear. Once again, another white, female yoga teacher adept taught the class. She was more approachable than the previous teacher had been. At this point, I was studying, practicing, and feeling good. I increased my commitment by joining a yoga community. Then something clicked: Yoga wasn't about the teacher; it was about my personal experience. The new teacher encouraged me to go beyond the asanas. Once I did, I knew that remaining the same person was no longer an option for me.

Despite all that I was learning and becoming, I still felt something was missing. Being the only African American in my classes made me wonder where I, as a woman of African descent, a woman of color, fit into this discipline? Why were there so few people of color in yoga? Did this spiritual practice, which felt so natural, exclude me? Could it be that African-American women felt intimidated by the asanas? Did yoga asanas bring up deep-rooted feelings about our bodies that we would rather hide? Did we understand what yoga could do for us? Or worse, did westernized yoga fail to address our unique circumstances, history, and subjugation?

To some, these questions may seem unsettlingly because times have changed. It is no longer the 16th century but 21st. We live in a post-racial era. By placing yoga within the context of historical and personal experiences, I am, in many ways, violating a code of silence concerning the relationship between our unique experiences and a culturally mindful yogic practice. Regardless of our experiences, we have been told to forget the past and live in the present. However, from my perspective, the unparalleled experiences of African-American women during the enslavement process are, in part, the reasons behind our personal suffering, disproportionate incidences of disease, and quality-of-life issues.

Our traumas and the chaos they cause are rooted in the discrimination, dehumanization, torture, and displacement of millions of African people. Our understanding of chaos must be at emotional level, not just an intellectual one. Chaos is an enduring and life-altering traumatic process. As with trauma, the question becomes, what do we do about chaos? Do we just forget about it or act as if it never existed, particularly when our very existence is a reminder of it?

Forgetting about trauma and chaos is not acceptable. Even if we choose not to remember, the damage done and consequences will not diminish. We can't wipe away the horrific experiences of the past. We have inherited the seeds of our ancestors' traumatic experiences, and these seeds give rise to our choices and behaviors. Our foremothers endured, but they suffered quietly. We are a part of them, and our suffering is naturally connected to their lives. Self-healing is the missing process of their experiences and ours. This healing must be channeled toward regaining wholeness and balance. Only then will we experience truth, justice, righteousness, and order.

A one-size-fits-all healing process will not work; we must understand our personal and cultural experiences for true transformation to occur. A generic psychology that embraces the ancient Greeks as our founding fathers will not work. Whether we refer to modern-day Sigmund Freud, or modern-day psychologist, we are neglecting African cosmology.

The theories, beliefs, and ideas of western psychology have often maligned the image of Africans. One example is the theories posited by Arthur Jensen, William Shockley, Richard Herrnstein, and Charles Murray. These psychologists wrote that blacks are genetically inferiority to whites based on IQ testing. As we explore western psychotherapy and psychology, with their sophisticated mental health classifications and accompanying medications, we find that the system is not designed to facilitate healing; instead, it maintains a state of disease and pathology. Western psychology's primary intervention is to dispense medication. It's no wonder that many people prefer to opt out of the system. Psychology and psychiatry do not offer effective treatments for the deep-seated fragmentation, uprootedness, and distortion Africans have experienced.

Based on my personal and clinical experience, yoga can counteract those horrific experiences by bringing balance and wholeness into our lives. Yoga predates our traumatic period. It's as if the divine intellect—the universe, Ra, Brahman, the All, Allah, God, Olodumare, Amun, and Nummo—gave us yoga as the prescription for healing. The question is, are we going to use yoga as an antidote so that we can reverse the effects of our experiences and return to our true selves? Many spiritual teachings tell us there's nothing we can do about the past; it's over. But if your past continues to be your present, then you must respond to the past. Some say, transcend the suffering. How do you transcend what you have not acknowledged or understood? How do you forget the pain and hurt when your life is a constant reminder of that pain and hurt? Have you ever experienced or knew someone who has been molested? Have you lost your parents or a loved one? Were your parents unfit or addicted to drugs? Have you ever had an abusive teacher? Have you ever been physically abused? Has your heart ever been broken? Our experiences between conception and birth shape our perceptions of ourselves and of the world.

As I learned later, our experiences define us either positively or negatively. When I was a child, I was beaten for walking on the wrong side of the street. One day, I was called "nigger;" the Catholic nuns at my school told me to forget about it. At work one day, I was asked what day was "kill a nigger day" and told it was a joke. I was told I had to be better than good if I wanted to keep my job. I didn't forget but I later found out the past can serve as the source of our healing.

As I continued my journey, I had the opportunity to advance my practice under a remarkable guru or spiritual teacher. This time, while I studied the yoga sacred texts I also began to explore Kemetic yoga. I read a book by Dr. Muata Ashby called *Egyptian Yoga: Movements of the Gods and Goddesses* (2005). As I read about the Egyptian yoga system, which had its own language, philosophy, and movements, I felt like I'd found a large sum of money. Words like Smai *Tawi* ("Yoga") and *Neter Metu* ("Divine Speech") drew me to yoga as a healing process. As I reflected on my findings, I began to feel good. For me, this ancient practice simply affirmed the connection between modern-day yoga and ancient Africa. In my studies, I saw poses that were similar to the classical yoga poses although the names were different. I researched Kemetic yoga and African cosmology but could find little on the subject. I studied the poses, the process, and the purpose of Kemetic yoga. Each pose was connected to a deity and to a story of healing and transformation. I learned from the ancient Kemetic text that our ancestors practiced yoga long before it arrived in India. Why had I not been taught this information? I spent an inordinate of time researching Kemetic yoga and found more insights but not at the level of Dr. Ashby's work. Meanwhile, I studied the yoga sutras; the classical yoga text, the Upanishads; a compilation of philosophical texts; the *Bhagavad Gita*; a 700–verse dharmic scripture; and Hatha Yoga which emphasizes a balanced, holistic yoga path. Ultimately, I felt most inspired by an ancient style of yoga practiced in ancient Africa that connects us to the gods and goddess by making us whole.

I discovered that the ancient Egyptians, who are the fathers and mothers of civilization, included yoga as a system of holistic wellness. Evidence of the similarities between ancient African practices and the yoga practices in ancient India has been documented by Edward Bruce Bynum (1999) and Muata Ashby (2001). However, despite the political and historical nature of how yoga arrived in the West, one simple truth excited me: Our African ancestors practiced yoga. Yoga as a healing and transformative practice is our birthright, our inheritance, and a divine gift that can awaken us.

I am awakened.

The Simple Truth

*I write to keep in contact with our ancestors
and to spread truth to people.*
—Soni Sanchez

Traditional yoga is an ancient practice. Few people know that it began in Africa more than two-million years ago. Long before other earlier civilizations our African ancestors practiced yoga, which included a dietary regimen, self-study, meditation, and asanas. Proof of this can be found on papyrus, temple walls, and statues. According to Dr. Muata Abhaya Ashby and Dr. Karen Ashby in *The Egyptian Yoga: Movements of the Gods and Goddesses*, yoga has been a discipline of self-awareness, self-knowledge, and self-actualization for human development since 300 BCE or earlier. As people from other regions became familiar with yoga's healing and transformative power, it spread to other parts of the world, most notably to India.

After some time, our ancestors' knowledge became codified in diverse languages and faded from our consciousness. Meanwhile, our encounters with that unimaginable trauma undoubtedly left a scar. For some people, it's difficult to imagine that ancient Africa gave the world the spiritual practice of yoga, which is seen as a blueprint for health, healing, and happiness today, but it did. Many of us have grown up hearing Africa referred to as the "dark continent," a place devoid of intellect, psychology, philosophy, art, or beauty.

Far too many African Americans perceive Africa as worthless. It's easy to see why we shun the birthplace of humanity. Consider the hideous media and textbook images that portray Africa as a continent of poor, starving people; illiteracy and poor educational systems; HIV/AIDS-ravaged bodies; and absolute suffering. Consider how little we know about Africa's positive influence on the arts, science, astrology, mathematics, music, deep thought, philosophy, and religion.

The contributions of ancient Africa to the practice of yoga must no longer be ignored. Mother Africa delivered from her womb a symphony of natural laws and spiritual systems that have been expressed under different guises and embedded in different cultures. Yoga students typically learn about India's ancient deities, such as Shiva, Parvati, Vishnu, Shakti, and Ganesha, and the eight limbs of Patanjali, the yoga sutras, the *Upanishads*, the Vedic texts, the *Mahabharata*, the *Puranas*, and the *Bhagavad Gita*. Such knowledge is, of course, necessary. However, it is historically inaccurate to present yoga as connected only to India. The presence of African deities—such as Amun, Ra, Olodumare, Heru Khuti, Aset, Esu, Tehuti, Maat, Ogun, Shango, and Osumare— has been unconsciously (or perhaps purposefully) omitted from contemporary yoga philosophy. People often ignore the deep thoughts of the sage Ptahhotep, who wrote the oldest textbook in human history. Unless someone seeks out Ptahhotep's *The Teaching of Ptahhotep*, *Divine Word*, *Book of Coming Forth by Day*, *Papyru of Ani* and the *Mystery Systems*, he or she will not know of their existence. No one can deny the seminal role India played in popularizing yoga;

however, Mother Africa, the source of civilization, was the source and the deliverer of yoga to the world.

To embrace this simple truth we must be willing to exhale the falsehoods and inhale the truth. Sometimes before we can let something into our lives, we must let something go. In other words, we have to unlearn to learn. If we desire to heal from our past, then the first step is truth.

Healing—which means to be or become whole or to create harmony—begins with the truth. How can we heal if what we believe about ourselves is false? How can we heal if we don't know who we are? How can we heal if we believe materialism is happiness, sex is love, and blue contact lenses will make us beautiful? How can we heal if we ignore the abuses in our lives? How can we heal if we are constantly stressed? Most importantly, how can we heal when we've been conditioned not to love ourselves, when deep down we feel inferior and unattractive because of the color of our skin and the texture of our hair? How can we heal if we feel privileged because we have lighter skin and straighter hair? Do you pause when someone asks you if you are black? How many of us have felt unwanted because we've been told we were too dark? Have you ever been asked, "Is that your hair?" as if it makes a difference? How many of us have never heard the words, *You are beautiful*?

Healing is only possible if we rediscover and acknowledge our true identities and our undeniable beauty, which explicitly reveal that Africa is the origin of humanity. Caroline Shola Arewa writes, "DNA tests indicate that all humans alive today are descended from a single female ancestor who lived in Africa 140,000–280,000 years ago." What does that say? Africa holds within her womb concepts, deep thoughts, philosophies, and practices that have spanned the world. If we view ourselves as seeds embodying African cosmology, then we must transcend our conditioning and connect to rituals, belief systems, and practices of healing.

Àse yoga is an inspired healing practice that draws from African science that states that wellness, healthiness, and happiness comes from our life-force and our knowledge of the self. Through a process of self-discovery, Àse yoga embraces healing as an answer to the transatlantic enslavement catastrophe and personal challenges.

We become what we believe. If we believe that we have nothing to offer humanity, then we will go through life feeling a sense of self-loathing. In Àse yoga, we acknowledge, understand, and transcend this trauma, this disillusion, which I believe we are still processing. Furthermore, this practice opens the path for us to overcome our personal mayhem and unmet needs, which results in disease, unhealthy parenting, misery, immorality, overconsumption, irresponsibility, insecurity, and unwise choices.

In response to our historical trauma and personal challenges, *The Art of Feeling Good* propose as a solution: the balancing power of Àse yoga. This practice believes that achieving self-knowledge unveils our true and long-forgotten identity and is the key to health and healing. As we move toward authenticity, we also discover that our relationship to an ancient African cosmology is one of the greatest unspoken realities. It holds precious gems in the form of universal truths about our glorious pre-enslavement existence. When we identify with our true selves, we will no longer answer to what others call us—colored, negro, black, wench, baby mama, or even bitch. Instead, we will answer to our divine identities as goddesses.

I feel authentic.

The Unveiling

We must wake up and take on the lifetime
responsibility for reaching our fullest potential
mentally, spiritually and physically.
—Asa G. Hilliard III

The word yoga comes from the Sanskrit root *yuj*, which means to yoke, link, and unite. Yoga is the unification of the individual self with the universal soul. Dr. Muata Ashby cites an article in *Yoga Journal* that states the origin of yoga occurred in India around the 9th century by Guru Gorakshanath. According to *Yoga Body: The Origin of Modern Posture Practice* by Mark Singleton, yoga asanas can even be traced from India to Europe as exercise absent the principles of personal and community development.

I couldn't help but wonder what role Africa played on the yoga timeline. Despite the works of the sage Ptahhotep, who lived in the twenty-fifth century BCE, the involvement of yoga in ancient Africa is largely ignored. In my studies, I found no mention of yoga in Africa. The one exception was Dr. Ashby, who states that yoga was practiced in ancient Egypt from 1580 to 300 BCE and was known as *Sema(Yoga)* or *Smai Tawi (Union of the Two lands of Egypt)*, African yoga. *Sema* means the union with the gods and goddesses in cultivating enlightenment. Books such as *Yoga: The Greater Tradition* by David Frawley mention yoga in northern Africa or ancient Egypt. But the seminal works of Muata Ashby, Karen Ashby, Edward Bruce Bynum, and Caroline Shola Arewa yoga's existence in ancient Africa has been brought to the forefront.

Why is this important? In addition to believing that truth is crucial to any discussion, I also believe that the deep thoughts, ancient wisdom, remedies, and practices that came from Africa need to be unveiled and given their rightful gratitude. Our ancient deities—Wsr, Horus, and Aset—experienced a cacophony of emotions, including negativity, grief, disappointment, and fragmentation in their lives. This cacophony of emotions ultimately culminated in unity and wholeness, or yoga. The struggles of Horus, the son of Wsr and Aset, were a representation of life. What happened to Horus, Wsr, and Aset is worthy of our study and understanding, just as is the *Bhagavad Gita*. How do we transform our struggles, obstacles, and challenges into healing? How do we attain wholeness? By practicing yoga because it holds the key to wholeness, compassion, power, wisdom, and, above all, love.

This phenomenon of yoking or union presupposes that we encounter life experiences that disconnect us from our original source, our root. What is more dissociative than denying who you are? What is more isolating than the psychological, emotional, social, economic, and physical disturbances we experience? What is more disruptive than the childhood tragedies we endure?

Dissociative statements include, *I'm not African, I don't know anything about Africa, I'm Jamaican, I'm Puerto Rican, I'm Native American, I'm Welsh,* and *I'm biracial.* What ethnic group other than Africans born in America repeatedly denies its relationship to its place of origin? Some African Americans say, *I don't know anything about Africa;*

therefore I'm not African. Others see Africa as undesirable and Africans as unattractive. In general, we, along with our children and our children's children, repudiate our heritage because of a lack of self-knowledge. Meanwhile, other groups express their culture through food, dress, philosophy, ritual, and celebrations. Too often, African Americans see themselves as culturally bankrupt or cultural orphans.

We have been conditioned to be at war with ourselves through the systematic dehumanization of the African born in America, the colonization of people on the African continent, and the fragmentation and disconnection from our roots. However, when we look at our health, social, psychological, and spiritual problems, it is clear that our ancestors foresaw that the effects of our bondage would call for the self-healing practice that is called yoga.

In the 21st-century, amidst capitalism and westernization, the practice of yoga has become synonymous solely with physical poses (asanas) or gymnastics. Most people identified as yogis look more like body builders or models, which sends the wrong message about yoga. People say they "do" rather than "practice" yoga. In one breath they say, "I do zumba, lift weights, and a little yoga." These statements misrepresent yoga as a physical activity that is only for the fit. In general, yoga has been cast as a display of poses people achieve rather than a representation of love, transformation, and healing.

Instinctively, we compare ourselves to the picture or the pose rather than to the process. How many of us have gone into a yoga studio and experienced the sequence of poses but not the function of yoga? Perhaps you have taken a yoga class and wondered what it was all about. Headstands, backbends, and twists become transient physical experiences rather than powerful spiritual answers to inner turmoil. Did you know that meditation and breath awareness are the mainstays of yoga? Meditation and breath awareness are mainstays of yoga. They are powerful tools, but they are not as easy to market as being toned, having a firm buttock, and sculpting the body is.

Often, yoga teachers show off their abilities by highlighting their students' inabilities. Physicality is emphasized at the expense of yoga's potent self-healing possibilities.

In addition, the images in popular yoga magazines are enough to frighten most people away. Shots of yogis and yoginis twisting and turning their bodies suggest that only highly agile, muscle-bound men and model-like, small, and flexible women can practice yoga, not you. Your mind tells you that the pictures are nice, but that activity is not for you.

If you thumb through those magazines, watch television, or visit one of the more popular yoga studios, you might think that yoga is solely a bodybuilding exercise with movements and poses for athletes. It may seem like yoga is only for people who are skilled at doing the poses. People travel far to learn the techniques, insights, and poses to give themselves the credentials to be yogis. How did our ancestors manage without frequent-flyer miles or yoga certification programs? With spiritual guidance, they turned inward and relied on stillness and meditation.

Some people might think that only Hindus, people with money, people who have traveled to India, people who have practiced for a number of years, and people who proudly refer to their gurus or teachers can become yogis. This is not the case. Even if you have never set foot outside of your neighborhood or do not feel flexible, you can be a yogi.

Yoga is a personal, inner experience that involves reconnecting and awakening to our divine nature. No amount of travel can ordain you as a yogi. It's about how you live and the choices you make. Yoga is a daily activity. By practicing yoga on a regular basis, we unite our individual or human consciousness with a higher or divine consciousness or enlightenment.

What is a higher conscience? To me, it is thinking divinely, not worrying, feeling whole, being creative, loving, and, above all, being authentic. When we are enlightened, we change the way we eat, live, and take care of ourselves, and we feel good.

When we become yogis, we do not make the same choices about our lives. We no longer resort to indiscriminate sexual behaviors, work just for money, consume useless items, or contaminate our senses with toxic sounds, thoughts, and associations. We undergo a metamorphosis that does not simply happen through poses.

The movements in yoga are only three-eighths of the journey; yoga provides access to a higher awareness. Steps within yoga lead to the development of social and personal principles, the divine order, physical discipline, breath awareness, sense withdrawal and peace of mind, concentration, meditation, and the ultimate union with the divine self. These principles are integral to the process and practice of yoga. Most people know of these principles as *yamas* and *niyamas*, the first two steps of the eight limbs of Patanjali. In African cosmology, these principles are known as Maat, named for the ancient Egyptian goddess of truth, balance, order, law, morality, and justice. Order exists in the universe and within us because of Maat.

Magazine pictures distract us from understanding the deeper meaning and benefits of yoga. The same is true of marketing strategists who use contortionist poses to sell yoga clothes and accessories. Because of these conflicting messages, our bodies go one way and our minds another. Yoga is like a thirsty person holding a glass of purified water but not drinking it. The person misses the amazing physical, spiritual, and mental benefits because he or she will not drink the water.

Because I had already experienced cancer, "the big C," the practice of yoga felt like a reunion. People often asked me how long had been practicing. I liked to respond that I had been practicing for a lifetime. It evolved organically inside of me. Because of the challenges I had experienced in my life, yoga wasn't theoretical, scholarly, or intellectual; it was emotional. Each pose released more and more tension, calmed my nervous system, and signaled my whole body to let go. Beyond the poses, however, becoming a yogini meant reflecting, meditating, and understanding my life experiences on a deeper level for the purpose of self-actualization. That encouraged me to want to know who I am and what my purpose is.

The first thing I did was detach from the overwhelming commercialization that surrounded me and connect to the practice of wholeness and healing. Such experiences are rare because yoga has become about the outward display of scantily clad bodies performing gymnastics or flexing muscles. We feed the Western appetite with the illusion of perfection by turning yoga into a performance rather than a practice.

I ask that you ignore what you see on magazine covers. It's an illusion. Yoga is natural medicine that promotes wellness, wholeness, and authenticity, which are vital to all beings. How much a yogi you are is not measured by how long you can stay in headstand, how taut your muscles are, how many sun salutations you can do, or how deeply you can fold forward. It's more profound than that. Yoga is consciousness, awareness, and ultimate transformation. When we engage in this ancient practice, we feel different. Our thinking and lifestyle change considerably. We finally feel good about ourselves. No longer do we reach for artificial stimulants, clog our senses with nonsense, or feel anxious, fearful and unmotivated. We don't endure diseases and depression as pastimes. By practicing yoga, we experience an awakening, a rebirth, and feelings of completeness.

I am whole.

Who Is Practicing Yoga?

When there is no enemy within, the
enemies outside cannot hurt you.
—African proverb

According to a 2008 *Yoga Journal* report, 15.8 million people practice yoga, 72.2 percent are women, and 71.5 percent are college educated. If you go into most yoga studios, you probably will find maybe one African-American woman. There may be more African-American teachers, but there is still a dearth of African-American women students. Perhaps we don't see ourselves and that's what keeps many African-American women away from yoga. Or maybe it is because of a lack of exposure to and misinformation about yoga. Or perhaps some African-American women believe that yoga is something that "white people do."

In my travels, I've met many African-American women who say that they want to practice yoga but don't have the time or aren't flexible enough. Those who attend class do it sporadically or in between relationships; others promise to go but never do. A health or emotional crisis can attract an African-American woman to yoga, as if it were an emergency room. As I listened to their excuses and their lists of psychological, spiritual, and stress-related problems, it became apparent to me that many of these women did not see yoga as a healing practice but merely as physical exercise. More importantly, many women did not see themselves as yoginis. They were not familiar with our illustrious African history and beautiful culture.

More white females practice yoga than African-American females, just as more females practice than males. However, it is important to make a distinction between taking a regular asana class and committing to a yoga practice or community. For some women, engaging in numerous asanas is the extent of their yoga experience; others embrace a yoga practice that leads them toward self-actualization and transformation.

The word practice suggests a pattern of activity. As a pattern, yoga includes more than movement. We often use the word yoga as a synonym for poses, but when we practice yoga as a lifestyle we think, act, and behave differently. When performed on a regular basis, yoga changes how we interact with the world, calms the nervous system, improves heath, reduces stress, and strengthens and heals the body and mind. We must understand that the practice is not the poses; the poses are a part of the practice.

I've known yoga teachers who are quite skilled in executing poses but are imbalanced in their personal lives or inexperienced teachers. Being a yoga teacher in the West is more about certification than initiation. After a few weeks or months of classes, someone can refer to himself or herself as a certified or registered teacher without having had training in the higher aspects of yoga. Becoming a yogi or yoga teacher is an initiation that cannot be bought.

When the student is ready, the master appears. Open yourself to infinite possibilities for feeling good. Practice what you want to see repeated. Be ready to become whole, balanced, and responsible. Seek authenticity with yoga. In return, you will receive an invaluable gift.

Perfect practice makes perfect.

If Not Yoga, Then What?

Religion kept some of my relatives alive, because it was
all they had. If they hadn't had some hope of heaven,
some companionship in Jesus, they probably would
have committed suicide, their lives were so hellish.
—Octavia Butler

I f we are not practicing yoga, then what are we doing? Some of us attend churches, mosques, or temples. Others take classes in belly, pole, or line dancing; zumba; or spinning. Some of us powerwalk. Some shop, take cruises, or go on extravagant vacations. Too few of us practice yoga as a lifestyle.

A number of reasons exist as to why more African-American women do not consistently practice yoga. An informal survey of one hundred women at the Àse Yoga Studio found that women gave the following reasons for why they did not practice yoga: time, money, distance, flexibility, religion, lack of exposure, and uncertainty due to religious affiliation. Among these money ranked the highest. According to a study published by the Wake Forest University Baptist Medical Center in June 2009, 31 percent of African-

American women admitted that they exercised *less* because they worried it might damage their hairstyles.

In my casual conversations and observations, religion and relationships also ranked high. Too many African-American women believe that yoga conflicts with their religion, even though it doesn't conflict at all. Several women told me that their churches teach that yoga *is* the antithesis of religion. Interestingly, few saw a conflict between sexual promiscuity or dishonesty and their religion. One woman debased yoga because of her strong Christian belief. Later, I found out that she saw nothing wrong with sleeping with married men. Another woman who appeared quite nervous attended yoga classes even though it went against her church's doctrine. After her class, she said that she felt better. I've noticed several women who view religious attire as an obstacle to practicing yoga, yet their behavior did not reflect their clothing in certain environments. Several women said that their churches told them not to practice yoga but gave no reason why. Some women believe that chanting will conjure up spirits. I don't know where this myth came from, but it's real. (Never mind that chanting occurs in other religious, political, and sports venues.) Chanting is used to evoke actions or feelings. It is clear that in the name of religion our lives are filled with contradictions.

Why do we separate our behaviors from our religious belief? How do we become whole? Why do we justify infidelity, drug abuse, fornication, anger, hypocrisy, self-depreciation, lying, deception, meanness, egotism, contradictions, and other sordid behaviors as long as we attend church, a mosque, or temple and contribute to charity? How many of us have compromised our religious beliefs during a relationship only to return when the relationship ends?

Whether Christian or Muslim, we hold our religious belief systems near and dear. In 2008, the Pew Forum on Religion and Public Life found that of all the major racial and ethnic groups in the United States, black Americans were most likely to report a formal religious affiliation. That study further indicated that nearly four out of five African Americans (79 percent) said religion is very important in their lives, compared with 56 percent of White Americans.

In terms of religion, I can also reflect on my personal experience. I was raised as a Catholic and was repeatedly told that Catholicism was the one true religion. On Saturday, I went to confession. On Sunday, I attended church. I studied the Catechism instead of *The Bible*. I believed sincerely that anyone who was not a Catholic would burn in hell. I had a supreme sense of superiority because I belonged to the one real religion: Catholicism. In my mind, Catholics were simply better than Protestants. In Catholicism, premarital sex was forbidden but people had premarital sex, with or without contraceptives.

I became somewhat of an expert in the nuances of religion. In later years, I witnessed numerous contradictions and even trauma within the church, which encouraged me to seek rather than simply accept. I uncovered a gem in *From the Browder Files*, which stated that the "term religion comes from the word RE which means *back* and *LIGON* which means to *HOLD* or to *BIND*." Is it possible that all religions really link us "back to the source of creation? Or Divine Soul?" What is that source? It is Divinity, which has many names and attributes. Religion is a highly sensitive issue, but I humbly ask you, *What's wrong with transforming or becoming a better human?* Is there something sinful about experiencing divinity? Shouldn't we take responsibility for our spiritual development and our health? Why shouldn't we seek a way to cease harming others or ourselves and experience peace?

Yoga does not conflict with religion. On the contrary, yoga compliments and even strengthens religious choice by improving concentration, focus, and discipline while leading us to wholeness and enlightenment. We understand prayer, but how many times have we prayed when our minds were on something else? When we pray while we practice yoga, we don't just go through the motions. We pray wholeheartedly. Praying is about the function and not simply the form. Besides, what's wrong with being healthy, happy, and whole?

Male-female relationships rank high on our list of priorities. Some women compromise their religion for their relationships but will not take a yoga class. We talk ad nauseam about our boyfriends, husbands, and lovers, and expend our energy trying to change someone into the person we want him to be. We've all been at least one of these women: the long-term girlfriend, the main girlfriend, the devoted girlfriend, the groupie, the unfaithful girlfriend, the drug-dealer woman, the wife, the insecure wife, the jilted girlfriend, the must-be-married woman, the woman on the side, the woman in between relationships, the long-distant lover, the one night stand, the sex partner, the girlfriend-in-waiting, and the infamous baby momma. In the end, our relationships validate us; without them we feel unhappy. It's as if we are constantly acting out the section in Alice Walker's *The Color Purple* when Shug says, "I's married now!" Once she has a husband to present to her father, Shug feels accepted. We go to great lengths to be accepted by waiting on someone who is already married or emotionally unavailable. We care for someone more than we care for ourselves.

Some of us even operate on the adage, *A piece of a man is better than no man at all.* One woman said that the men in her family are henpecked and the women are mean and controlling. She said, "It's deep. It goes back to my grandparents. My grandfather was abusive to my grandmother and his children. In turn, my grandmother became abusive to my mother and her siblings." This woman spent a great deal of energy trying to safeguard her relationships from the inevitable: infidelity. Yet it happened several times over. She was trying to make sure that her boyfriends didn't cheat on her. Often she was angry, not about what was actually happening but about what she thought might be happening. An extremely talented artist, she neglected her craft and tried to control something she could not control. You cannot control or change another person. Eventually, it will make you sick.

As if addicted, we sometimes do just about anything to hold onto our relationships, even if it means abandoning our friends and the healing process. When we are in a relationship, we tend to put all of our energy into sustaining it, often at the expense of taking care of ourselves or making wise choices for our lives. Some women have learned from their mothers to choose mates based on money, status, and even appearance rather than who a person is inside.

We've been bamboozled into thinking that sex is love. It's physical; it's earthly. But it never lasts. Love is not needy, lustful, or begging. Love is peace. We're stuck in loveless relationships when we don't know what love is. We've settled for sex instead of love. Taste the sweetness and smell the fragrance of real love. Let go of your expectations. Maybe you will taste the sweetness and smell the fragrance of real love.

Often women attend a few yoga classes and then stop coming. For some, yoga is a way-station on the road to a relationship. For others, it is a whim until the relationship ends, a crisis occur, or a doctor recommends a yoga class. As the saying goes, *If we knew back then what we know now, then our choices might have been different.* The choices we make when we are asleep are different from those we make when we are awake. Yoga is transformative; therefore, the person you attract without it may not be the person you attract with it. Are you willing to let go of an unhealthy relationship and embrace an authentic relationship with yourself and a spiritual relationship with others?

Then there is the money concern. Women say they don't have the money for yoga, but they have money to spend on their hair, nails, and other nonessentials. According to a BET survey called "African Americans Revealed" (2010), black buying power is at about $913 billion and is projected to increase to $1.2 trillion by 2013. Some estimates indicate that within five years, black households will spend more than $1 trillion each year. "Respect Black" (February 2012) reports indicate that African-American women spend $7 billion to $8 billion on cosmetics alone. According to a P&G/*Essence* poll, the average black woman spends three times as much on beauty products compared with the average woman. We have money, but we don't have money. This is not to deny that disparities and social injustices exist in healthcare coverage, access to education, and other quality of life issues. What we spend our money on is to awaken us to become more personally responsible and conscious to change the things that we can, particularly ourselves.

What do we value? Could it be that yoga has no market value in our community? Perhaps we don't see value in Western yoga because it has been so masterfully marketed as a practice of exclusivity rather than inclusivity. I believe that if we experience yoga's positive effect on our lives we will commit some of the more than $836 billion we have in total earning ability on healing from the inside, taking care of ourselves, being in healthy relationships, and becoming self-realized and self-actualized.

Yoga heals.

Who Are We?

*If the first woman God ever made was strong
enough to turn the world upside down all alone,
these women together ought to be able to turn
it back, and get it right side up again!*
—**Sojourner Truth** (1797? – 1883)

Who are we? We are nineteen million women strong, which makes us a valuable 7 percent of the US population. We are mothers, wives, co-wives, paramours, mistresses, daughters, aunts, in-laws, foster mothers, nieces, sorors, sisters, and grandmothers. We greet each other as sisters and queens, with peace but also, at times, with derogatory names. Our roles range from serving as the first lady of the United States to working girls. Although some of us have no children, others have several. We are high-school dropouts and high-school graduates. Some of us have bachelor's degrees; others have PhDs. We are doctors, secretaries, judges, home healthcare aides, professors, models, editors, surgeons, detectives, nurses, nursing assistants, garbage collectors, cleaning ladies, lawyers, journalists, actresses, welfare recipients, psychologists, fire fighters, college students, waitresses, entrepreneurs, university presidents, wardens, guards, receptionists, entertainers, inmates, scientists, teachers, writers, hairstylists, pole dancers, police officers, daycare owners, educators, health technicians, retirees, accountants, social workers, and much more. We are rich, ghetto-rich, middle class, and poor. We are single, married, divorced, engaged, and widowed. We are Christians, Muslims, believers, Spiritualists, nation-builders, Afro-centrists, priestesses, queen mothers, traditionalists, and activists. We are young and old, but we are also elders. We have boyfriends, paramours, husbands, and lovers. In some cases, they are philanderers.

There is diversity in what we look like, what we do, where we live, how we think, what we have and want, and with whom we sleep. That diversity shapes our lives. When all is said and done, our shared, collective experience connects us in a way that no one can deny. Our collective experience makes us smile with First Lady Michele Obama and shake our heads at the black woman being carted off to prison. Although our roads have taken different paths, we started at the same place and we take our triumphs and tragedies to heart.

We are the great granddaughters of African women who lived, fought, and killed in enslavement but died as freewomen. We are the byproducts of molestation and submission. We arose from the labor pains of Jezebels and Mammies. We are the seeds of the African women who fought on the quarterdeck during the Middle Passage. We are freedom fighters on board slave ships. We are the descendants of African women who were bred by force. We are the children of the children who ran away from the plantation.

We've come a long way since 1444, the beginning of the slave trade; however, along the way, we've forgotten who we were. We've forgotten that 200,000 years ago, an African woman was the maternal ancestor of every human being on the planet (Wilson et. al. 1985). Because we have lost that memory, we spend a good portion of our lives adapting rather than reclaiming, living the lie rather than embracing the truth, and looking good rather than feeling good.

We call ourselves Robbin, Beyoncé, Diane, Carol, Patricia, Lucille, Gladys, Linda, and Michele. Really, we are queens: Nzinga, Ankhenesmerire, Aset, Yaa Asantewa, Hatshepsut, Hypatia, Nyame, Atopoapoma, Astou, Maat, Oshepotu, Nisa Ra, Hathor, Nefertiti, and Cleopatra. If we only knew who we were, L'Oreal would not be able to define us as French or Creole. It would not be acceptable for entertainers to switch race for marketing purpose or black comedians to poke fun at our sensitivities. Skin-whitening creams would not exist. Our daughters' hair would no longer be our preoccupation. We'd cease to judge ourselves by the length of our hair or size of our derrieres; instead, we'd focus on the quality of our lives. In doing so, our daughters would be able to avoid our diseases and the burdens we carry. In self-acceptance, there would be no identity conflict because being an African woman would suffice.

What does this have to with yoga? Practicing yoga wakes you up. Jokes and disparaging remarks about African-American women are no longer funny. You no longer support entertainment that does not serve you. As Dr. Paris Finner-Williams stated at the Association of Black Psychology Conference (2010), you stop doing permanent things with temporary people in your life. With yoga, you begin to love and accept yourself. You understand your challenges and commit to healing. When you practice yoga, your true self emerges. You let go of whatever past traumas disconnected you from your essence. You experience life.

Be yourself.

What Is Going On?

*The greatest gift is not being afraid
to question.—Ruby Dee*

I n spite of our materialism, capacity to spend money, altered looks, vacations, and high-level positions, African Americans are more likely than other groups to be afflicted with certain diseases. Something in our lives makes us experience disease and death at a disproportionate rate. *The Art of Feeling Good* through the power of Àse yoga changes that situation.

Stay with me. Don't become defensive or angry about what you are about to read. Don't dismiss it as negative talk or simply deny it. Examine yourself or your family members. Is anyone suffering from poor health? This part of the journey will highlight the health aspects of our lives. I often hear remarks about moving beyond the data on health disparities for black women and focusing on intervention. If the data stays the same or worsens, it speaks to the effectiveness of efforts to reduce or eliminate the mortality rates for black females. This book grew out of my desire to be a part of that positive change and motivate African-American women to wake up, take care of themselves, and become personally responsible.

Reports from the *Heart Healthy Women* and the *New York Times* (2012) indicate that more than 40 percent of African-American women experience hypertension. Most likely, you or someone you know has been diagnosed with this disease. With hypertension, the heart has to work harder to pump blood, which can lead to organ damage and several illnesses. *Net Wellness Consumer Health Information* (2012) reported that 20 percent of African-American women with high blood pressure will die because of it. The Office of Minority Health in the US Department of Health and Human Services (2011) reported that even though African-American adults are 40 percent more likely to have high blood pressure, they are 10 percent less likely than their non-Hispanic white counterparts to keep their blood pressure under control. African-American women with hypertension are more likely to have other serious problems, such as stroke, heart disease, and kidney failure. Do you know anyone with these conditions?

Some of us believe it is a stigma to have high blood pressure. An estimated 27 percent of African Americans do not even know they have high blood pressure. We live with untreated symptoms until something happens. We tell ourselves that despite the systolic and diastolic numbers, we don't have high blood pressure. We say that we feel all right, forgetting that's why high blood pressure is called the "silent killer." What is your blood pressure on average?

Still not convinced that you need to change your life? Reportedly, heart disease is twice as high among African-American women than among white women. The National Coalition for Women with Heart Disease reports that the rate of heart disease among African-American women is 72 percent higher than it is for white women. African-American women ages fifty-five to sixty-four are twice as likely as white women to have a heart attack, and 35 percent of African-American adults are likely die from heart disease.

Did you know strokes are twice as high among African-American women than they are among white women? African-American women also have a higher risk of dying from a stroke than do white women. How can we continue to ignore these serious chronic disorders—hypertension, heart disease, and stroke—knowing that they affect us at a higher rate than any other racial group?

Stay with me. White women are slightly more likely to develop breast cancer than African-American women are. However, according to Breast Cancer.org, breast cancer is more common in African-American women under forty-five than in white women of the same age. The Black Women's Health Initiative (2009) reported that African-American women are 30 percent more likely to die of breast cancer than white women are. Although breast-cancer mortality rates have been declining among American women, black women appear to have a higher risk of developing deadly breast cancers early in life. Premenopausal black women are more than twice as likely to get an aggressive form of the disease. African-American women are less likely to have access to life-saving treatments. I was one of the exceptions; my cancer was detected during my annual mammogram.

My mother and many of my family members died from diabetes. Fortunately, I have not been diagnosed with the disease. Many African-American families have someone with type 2 diabetes. Type 2 diabetes makes up ninety to ninety-five percent of all diabetes cases. In type 2 diabetes, the insulin the body produces is unable to perform its primary job to help the body's cells use glucose for energy. An article on womenshealth.gov (May 18, 2010) reported that 25 percent of African-American women over the age of fifty-five have type 2 diabetes. One in four African-American women older than fifty-five has diabetes. African Americans also have high rates of at least two of diabetes' most serious complications:

amputation and kidney failure. The Black Women's Health Imperative (blackwomenshealth.org) projects that almost half of all African-American females who were born during or since the year 2000 are at serious risk for type 2 diabetes. We can change these numbers.

We rarely talk about lupus, but lupus disproportionately affects women of color. According to the Lupus Foundation of America, lupus is three times more common in African-American women than in white women. Lupus is an immune-system disorder. Every now and then, you hear about a friend who is experiencing lupus. Rarely do we think it can affect us.

African Americans continue to experience higher rates of sexually transmitted diseases than any other race/ethnicity in the United States. Most of us exercise our right to be sexually active. According to the Black Women's Health Imperative, "African-American women account for 66% of new cases of HIV among women." Although African Americans represent only 12 percent of the US population, they represent 22 percent of Americans with Hepatitis C. How many of us ask our partners to wear a condom? A few men have said that most women don't even ask about condoms.

According to the Office of Minority Health, African-American women are more likely to be overweight compared to other groups in the United States. About four out of five African-American women are overweight. According to the Black Women's Health Imperative, about 80 percent of African-American women are overweight and nearly half are obese. This increases the risk of type 2 diabetes. The National Health Institute defines obesity as being thirty pounds over the normal weight for a person's height or a having a body mass index of thirty or more. WebMD cites obesity as being twenty pounds over one's normal weight. It is true that some people find the word "obese" derogatory, but no matter what it's called excess weight or body fat leads to disease.

For unknown reasons, black women have a much higher incidence of fibroids than white, Hispanic, or Asian women do. Fibroids are noncancerous growths, or normal uterine cells that begin to grow abnormally, that develop inside or just outside a woman's uterus or womb. According to the Philadelphia Black Women's Health Project, one study showed that fibroids are three times more common in African-American women than in Caucasian women. In addition, fibroids tend to be larger and occur at an earlier age in African Americans. Too often medical professionals say that fibroids are common in African-American women.

I wanted to know why. Recently, a team of researchers led by Dr. Lauren Wise of Boston University's Slone Epidemiology Center found strong evidence indicating that air relaxer increases the risk for uterine fibroid tumors because it exposes black women to various chemicals through scalp lesions and burns. Dr. Wise's team followed more than 23,000 premenopausal black American women between 1997 and 2009. The team published a study called "Hair Relaxer Use and Risk of Uterine Leiomyomata in African-American Women" in the online edition of the *Journal of American Epidemiology* (January 10, 2012).

Did you know that African Americans are three times more likely to die from asthma? In reference "Asthma: A Concern for Minority Populations" (2001), the Asthma and Allergy Foundation of America found that African-American women have the highest asthma mortality rate of all ethnic groups, more than 2.5 times higher than Caucasian women.

Are we angry or sad? Perhaps both. Depression and anxiety are common among African-American women. We talk without ever admitting what the problem really is. African Americans carry a heavy burden when it comes to depression because we are less likely than Caucasians to seek mental health services or to receive proper diagnoses and treatments. In "Lives of Women of Color Create Risk for Depression" (October 1, 2001), the authors indicate that

African-American women are more likely to have depression because of racism, gender bias, poverty, violence, large family size, and social disadvantages.

It's not unusual for someone to complain to her medical doctor about symptoms that sound like depression, only to be diagnosed with attention deficit hyperactivity disorder (ADHD). Nowadays, ADHD is a default diagnosis. When doctors don't know what something is or they prefer not dig deeper into the issue, they call it ADHD. I've seen some women go through life accepting their physician's label of ADHD and taking medicine for a nonexistent diagnosis.

Let's look at crime. FBI statistics point out that a woman is battered every fifteen to eighteen seconds in the United States. African-American women suffer deadly violence from family members at rates decidedly higher than other racial groups. These statistics show that African-American women experience sexual assaults at an alarming rate and often are victimized at a very young age. Due to a variety of factors, it is difficult for them to get the therapeutic support they need. According to an ongoing study conducted by Black Women's Blueprint in which more than three hundred black women nationwide participated, 60 percent of black girls experience sexual abuse before they reach the age of eighteen.

In the *Madam Noire* article "Number of Young African-American Women in Prison Rises" (March 16, 2011), Charlotte Young states that the fastest growing incarcerated population in the country is composed of African-American girls and young women. There are now more women than ever serving time, and black women make up a disproportionate number. Think of them of as your daughters, your daughters' friends, your neighbors, and your family members, not just as a number. Then maybe this statistic will enrage you. A consequence of the incarceration population is that 1.7 million children, more than 70 percent of which are children of color, have a parent in prison.

Today, substance abuse disorders continue are on the rise, especially in the African American community. In "African Americans, Substance Abuse and Spirituality" (2004) published in *Minority Nurse*, Alice B. Britt writes that African Americans comprise approximately 12 percent of the population in the United States, yet in 1999 they accounted for 23 percent of admissions to publicly funded substance-abuse treatment facilities.

We've heard some of these statistics on the news, in conversation, and on the radio and television. Still, the numbers do not change. Whether we believe AIDS spreads via government manufactured, sexual contact, or by design, we have to be personally responsible for our health. . Being healthy is a personal responsibility that necessitates a change in our thoughts and actions. Change begins with us.

If it were not for accidents and emergencies, many of us would not set foot in medical care facilities. Some people attribute our distrust of the health-care system to the Tuskegee experiment. Between 1932 and 1972, doctors in Tuskegee, Alabama studied the natural progression of syphilis in poor, rural black men by denying them treatment under the pretext that they were receiving free health care from the US government. We also live in a society that has devalued the lives of Africans throughout the diaspora. These governmentally and socially sanctioned behaviors affect our minds, self-perceptions, and behaviors.

We must not volunteer to be in a Tuskegee experiment for the 21st century and instead commit to a healthy lifestyle. How many of us postpone our annual checkups because every time we go to the doctor's office he or she finds something wrong? How many of us use over-the-counter remedies, ignoring the consequences associated with avoiding medical treatment? How many of us complain to our girlfriends about chronic pain for years without going to a doctor? How many of us fail to participate in our own health care?

Going to the doctor is not a passive process. You should be an active participant in sustaining your life force. You know your body. It sends out signals for hours, days, months, and sometimes years, but you don't heed its warning. MRI scans reveal that brain tumors are replacing one-fourth to half of the skull where viable brain tissue is now necrotic. I've known women endure fibroids the size of a three-month-old fetus, and diabetic patients as young as thirty receive preoperative consultations to amputate an extremity. Some are on their way to dialysis treatments due to kidney failure. For one woman, this hit close to home when a family member who suffered from diabetes, hypertension, and weighed four hundred pounds died at the age of forty-one. Her dad was forty-seven when he passed. We have to want to live. These extreme conditions do not occur overnight. Some of us are predisposed to certain illnesses, have acquired them congenitally, or have succumbed to an accident. Our response time and follow-up determines how physically, emotionally, and financially devastating a disease will become. Some women postpone medical exams because they have hair appointments, vacations, or other family "emergencies." They get blood work done but never ask for the results. What is more urgent than removing aggressively growing masses within our bodies?

Think critically. Do your research. Be cautious if someone tells you don't take vitamins or buy the latest grape juice fortified with vitamins Z. Don't take vitamins or buy the latest grape juice fortified with vitamin C. That may not be what your body needs. I would be not be alive today if I did what people told me to do when I was confronted with cancer.

Is it our fear, ignorance, or both that hinders our ability to deal with our health issues? Either way, when health-care concerns are not addressed, it doesn't mean they cease to exist. If we are to care for our loved ones, our communities, or ourselves we must be strong in mind, body, and consciousness.

When the red light on your dashboard reminds you to take your car in for a checkup, you make a mad dash to the mechanic. When your hair is not done, you leave work and head to the appointment. I ask you to ponder this question: why can't you do the same for the most important asset you possess—your body, mind, and spirit? Stop putting your health in the backseat. Health is wealth. Prevention is the key. Breath and food are your first lines of defense. Breathe completely. Eat to live. Listen to your body. It communicates with you. Remember, prevention is better than a cure.

We don't have to succumb to these statistics or merely survive. Let's disinherit our diseases. Through yoga, we begin the path of reunification with the needs of our bodies, minds, and spirits. In practicing yoga, we gradually change behaviors that no longer serve us. These behaviors, which may contribute to our health imbalances, include unhealthy lifestyles, harmful thoughts, procrastination, fear, congested energy centers, toxic relationships, and even enslavement memories buried within our subtle physiology. If we are in harmony with the universe and aware, then health is not an anomaly but a given. Have you ever seen the sun or moon sick? Yoga in its true form co-creates universal harmony, awareness, and health. Even if you went to the doctor and were told everything was all right, it would not mean you were healthy if you were out of balance. We must consider the experiences of our ancestors, foremothers, and forefathers and adopt a preemptive healing process that recognizes that something happened to create an imbalance. Our ancestors have given us yoga to restore balance; otherwise, we will transmit our imbalances to our children.

Take care of yourself.

Embracing Right Knowledge

When I was a child, it did not occur to me, even once
that the black in which I was encased (I called it brown
in those days) would be considered one day, beautiful.
—Gwendolyn Brooks

Some of us may feel perfectly healthy; others may be suffering from a chronic illness. *The Art of Feeling Good* is about the power within us to live a healthy, balanced, and peaceful life through the practice of Àse yoga. Because of our busy lifestyles, making yoga a priority may seem unfeasible. Distractions, materialism, and sensory stimulation delude us into thinking we have it together. From work, we go home, and from home, we go to work feeling unfulfilled.

We continue to neglect our deeper issues in life until things fall apart and situations don't go the way we want them. Then aches or life-threatening illnesses cause us to seek help. Relationships, divorce, parenting, grief, and finances may leave us feeling overwhelmed. Our responses may run the gamut from physical ailments to emotional distress that affects our energy levels, health, and emotional stability.

Nothing stays the same. Life is constantly changing. Yet we try to defy uncertainty. When a relationship or job ends for any reason, we suffer. If we delve deeper, we find that suffering comes from an array of experiences. One often-overlooked cause of suffering is our collective historical experience from the enslavement process that affected not only how we relate to one another but also ourselves.

We tend to dismiss historical experiences as things that happened long ago and unrelated to who we are now. Nothing could be further from the truth. The law of causation tells us there is a relationship between everything that happens and everything that follows. What happened yesterday and what happened three years ago have an effect on what happens today; it's all interconnected. Just look at children harmed by sexual abuse and ask if the harm goes away once they are adults.

Delving deeper into suffering, we see what our ancestors called chaos or uncertainty. Chaos, which is considered a natural aspect of life, disrupts order. Interestingly, though, huddling inside that chaos is regret and revelations. Chaos reveals something about us. I believe that extracting that message is critical to our wellness. One area of chaos for many of us is survival: having a job, making money, or not making enough money. Money issues can create quite a bit of turmoil. Is money really the issue when you don't work, can't sustain a job, or spend more money than you have? In my clinical experience, I've found that, regardless of our education level or financial status, money chaos relates to our block root energy force, which grounds us. In other words, money is a symptom of an energetic imbalance. Unfortunately, we tend to compensate or ignore the blockage.

We cannot have balance and meaningful lives without being grounded, connected, and centered in the world. We cannot become balanced simply by talking about our suffering or problems; we must actively seek balance and order by investing in a spiritual path. Otherwise, we will continue to replicate suffering and chaos. Telling a story repeatedly without a revelation only sustains the suffering.

Physical and emotional suffering and uncertainty in our lives is inevitable; yet for most of us suffering from the enslavement process is difficult to fathom. We've been programmed to dissociate from it. We prefer to discuss the historical nature of racism and discrimination or the civil rights movement on an intellectual level and remain silent about the enduring toll these experiences have on our mental and physical wellbeing.

I believe we are still processing the chaos from the enslavement process. Unfortunately, we have settled for chaos by accepting our lives as the way they are rather than fulfilling our true purpose. But what we ignore doesn't disappear.

In fact, one offshoot of that chaos may be our infamous attitude. That's right, we've been tagged with an attitude. People see us as having an attitude and tag us with the "angry black woman syndrome." Others believe that we are hostile toward others, society, and ourselves. At times, we are perceived as unapproachable. We also are known for rolling our eyes and moving our heads up and down in response to what someone said or did. On television and for money, we jump into character. Our necks pop and fingers snap. We act the way others expect us to act.

What do you think? Do we have an attitude or is it stereotyping? Women have shared with me their reluctance to go through a grocery store line if a black woman is the cashier. Are you reluctant to ask for customer service from one of your sisters? Do you travel out of the neighborhood just to avoid the "attitude"? Have you ever felt, thought or stated something derogatory toward another African-America female because of race? Has anyone ever said that you have an attitude?

What is an attitude? According Wikipedia, an attitude is a positive or negative reaction toward something or someone expressed in one's beliefs, feelings, or behaviors. It is an opinion that one has about someone or something.

The question is, how do you really feel about yourself? Are you happy? Have you ever felt the effects of racism or been mistreated? Did you ever think you were not offered a job because of the color of your skin? Were you a recipient of your mothers' disappointments? Do you dislike the way you look? Do you believe people from other ethnic groups have better lives than you do? Have you ever wished your nose was thinner, your hair straighter, or your skin lighter? Do you work hard to make others feel comfortable? Do you work harder than others to prove your worth and value on the job? Do you wish you were someone else? Has anyone ever said you are beautiful? The answers to these questions affect our attitudes toward others and ourselves. They fuel either feelings of chaos and suffering or self-love and confidence.

We did not just wake up one morning and decide to feel the way we do. Attitudes come from somewhere. How you feel about yourself is rooted in something that happened in the past. Experiences become deeply embedded in your mind and body, resulting not only in negative attitudes and anger but also fear, anxiety, unhappiness, and tension. This is when we need to ask the question, *Could my current choices be connected to my previous experiences?*

They are. What we call a negative attitude is actually a form of internal chaos that we ignore. Most of us go through life ignoring the effects that the experiences of our foremothers and forefathers had on us. Underneath our accomplishments is a struggle for acceptance at any cost. We are on guard and on edge because of a build up of unresolved stress.

We deny the problem. However, nothing replaces the emptiness, confusion, and pain from within. We try to act like nothing bothers us, but everything does. Deep inside, we feel insecure and afraid, disconnected, and unloved. Over the years, we have answered to many names, but all we want to know is, "Ain't I a woman?"

What is going on? As mentioned earlier, I believe our attitudes come from the enslavement process as well as our extraordinary personal challenges. Discrimination, dehumanization, rape, death, displacement, prejudice, castration, and defeminization have left negative scars that cause us to question who we are. Chaos expands itsel if left unresolved. How can we forget the rape, abuse, abandonment, neglect, incest, displacement, torture, and government-sanctioned racism when we are a direct result of those painful experiences? Self-healing is critical.

Imagine your mother, sister, aunt, or even you confined to a dark and low place, shackled in irons. Imagine your child being thrown over the side of a ship and eventually dying. Imagine having your arms broken while you are in shackles. Imagine being sold. Imagine being whipped, raped, and tortured. The enslavement process was a dehumanizing practice. It was not an event or a war; it was the barbaric capture of an estimated fifty million African people. Nothing can compare to the insidious cruelty that occurred in the United States, which left the enslaved to question their identities and self-worth because of their race.

In addition to the embedded historical stressors, our attitudes arise from personal experiences. We respond to assaults on our self-identify and self-worth by suppressing, compensating for, or disassociating from this tragedy. Some of us were displaced. Some were raised in unloving foster homes or by mentally unstable mothers. Others were exposed to drug addiction, incest, promiscuity, abandonment, alcoholism, depression, incarcerated parents, impoverishment, detached caretakers, divorces, religious dogma, philandering partners or spouses, physical and mental abuse, and mis-education. Those who have grown up with intact families still have to navigate through feelings of being associated with a race that has been considered less desirable than others. These experiences matter because they send a message about our self-worth and self-image. Who we are and why we are here are critical questions that we must answer. If we fail to do so, chaos flows from one generation to the next and into the individual, family, and community.

At present, few messages in our society make us feel good about who we really are. For the most part, what we see in the media leaves us yearning to be someone else. Beauty is defined as something other than what we are. When have you heard an African-American woman described as beautiful? Michele Obama, Angela Basset, Phylicia Rashad, and many other African-American women are beautiful but rarely are they described in that way. As a result, we spend our time trying to look like the popular depiction of beauty.

We risk a lot to achieve that ideal, even if it harms us. We hold our real feelings inside, because they are too uncomfortable to express. Some of us simply refuse to associate with anything that has to do with being African, whether it is enslavement or culture. Others push away unhappiness they cannot explain.

Seldom, however, do women consistently gather for healing. They gather for family reunions, baby showers, parties, malls, restaurants. They go to homecoming and make hospital visits. They buy luxury cars and designer bags and go on cruises. They go to hair and nail salons.

Only when something happens or we fall ill do we divulge one of our many little dirty secrets: domestic abuse, adoption/foster care, incest/rape, drugs, homicide, mental illness, abandonment, infidelity, and, more often than all others, heartbreak. Overcome with emotion, we share our pain. However, because of unbridled chaos we share *wrong knowledge*.

While studying *The Yoga Sutras of Patañjali*, this concept of wrong knowledge caught my attention. What if our struggles in life are the result of wrong knowledge? Wrong knowledge means that we misunderstand and misinterpret what is happening to us. It relates to how we think and act. For example, if I had been abused as a child, I might grow up to believe that all people will abuse or harm me. As a result, I might settle for situations that are abusive, which in turn validate my thinking. Because I mistrust others, I hold back and feel fearful and weighed down. The decisions and choices I make in life lead me to unhealthy relationships.

Wrong knowledge also creates illusions or false beliefs that we treat as real. Illusions are darkness. Even in the face of truth, we prefer to deny, escape, and ignore reality. Usually, when pressed, we respond by saying "whatever," as we cling to the misinformation. In doing so, we jeopardize our health and happiness and those of our community. An example of an illusion is the belief that AIDS no longer exists or that your partner does not have to wear a condom because he "looks clean." Another is that a man living with another woman is emotionally available for a relationship, or that if you are not tested for HIV, you will not be infected. Another example is that if your partner marries you, then everything will be all right. Another is that you will feel better if you keep doing the things that made you feel sick, depressed, and unmotivated in the past. Illusions affect how we think and feel. After a while, our environments, family structures, past experiences, mind-sets, and lifestyles reinforce these false beliefs.

With wrong knowledge, we do not see our own worth, beauty, and purpose, only what people say we are. Wrong knowledge is a function of the mind. To experience right knowledge we must shift our thinking. This change cannot come from medical doctors, pills, intoxicants, sex, escapades, or elixirs because they treat only the symptoms, not the mind. The latest rap or hip-hop song will not change our faulty thinking either. In the poignant words of Malcolm X, "We've been took! Hoodwinked! Bamboozled! Led Astray! Run amok!" into becoming what others want us to be. We do not believe in our beauty, intelligence, or femininity. Instead, we believe what we have been taught and exposed to, even though it is wrong knowledge. We have succumbed to the debasing messages in rap music, popular songs, tabloid articles, and other TV characters, forgetting that we are goddesses, queens, and mothers of civilization. Over the years, because of this lost memory, we've acted differently than our true selves, not as the royalty that we once were.

If we look inward, we will find extraordinary obstacles in the form of emotional responses, such as self-hatred, stress-related illnesses, fear of hell, disempowerment, low self-esteem, and disappointment. Our disdain over our full lips, thick hair, melanin, body image, nose shape, eyelashes, and hair length is a weighty issue. Wrong knowledge penetrates our thought processes so that some of us go so far as to biologically engineer our children so they're light skinned and not dark skinned. We don't want children that look like us. We trade in our uniqueness for commonality. Love is forfeited to physical looks. Far too many of us defer our aspirations, dreams, and creativity and inhibit our emotions and sexuality because of wrong knowledge. Despite our advanced degrees, titles, luxury cars, poodles, male acquaintances, upward mobility, and economic solvency, we walk around with an accumulation of heartbreak and self-perpetuated suffering, doubting our true worth.

If we operate on wrong knowledge, then whatever we do, however we act, is wrong. This way of thinking deludes us into settling instead of living, being with someone instead of loving him, and doing mindless work instead of living with purpose. We move from one toxic situation to another. We sacrifice precious time living under the guise of false beliefs. Often, we believe there is nothing we can do about it; however, nothing could be further from the truth.

Our traumatic experiences, early insecurities, unmet needs, fears, stressful lifestyles, and emotional challenges become our reality. We exist in survival mode, dealing with adversities and enduring extreme stress. We adopt a way of existing, not living that compromises our bodies and defers our happiness.

The cost of living this way is immeasurable. We become susceptible to disease and chronic illnesses, which are often stress-related and symptomatic of deeper issues in our lives. Compounding the problem, we deal with symptoms, not causes. Could our psychosomatic complaints, nervousness, insecurities, psychological imbalances, and chronic health complaints all stem from wrong knowledge?

Until I felt the pain of discontent, disease, and distress, I did what everyone else did. I lived in a less than authentic manner. I existed superficially in the shadow of life and went through the motions. I believed what I had been told, rather than what I had personally experienced. I existed in a box of finite possibilities. It took a life-threatening disease to usher me into the world of healing and energy.

When practicing Àse yoga, we give ourselves *right knowledge* to bring order to our chaos, experience happiness, and feel good. I invite you to experience the power of Àse yoga. In right knowledge, you will reach a state of self-realization, self-acceptance, and self-actualization. Love for your true self will emerge as you fulfill your unique purpose on Earth. No longer will you compare yourself to others. You will embrace your beauty, emancipate yourself, and transform.

I am free and beautiful.

Personal Responsibility

*I have come to believe over and over again
that what is most important to me must be
spoken, made verbal and shared, even at the
risk of having it bruised or misunderstood.*
—Audre Lorde

Transformation doesn't just happen; obstacles do exist. I've found that two obstacles inhibit our ability to live healthy and with purpose: thoughts and conditioning. How we think determines what we do or don't do; what we wear, do, or eat; where we go; how we relate to others; and how we spend our money. Our thinking fuels our actions. For instance, if we think with fear, our lives, relationships, careers, and friendships reflect that fear. This is because our thoughts create situations that either harm or enhance us.

The second obstacle, conditioning, sustains the enslavement process by limiting and confining us within a specific area. Our conditioning leads us to devalue our bodies, attach to unhealthy lifestyles, and accept less than we deserve. Our conditioning and thought patterns affect the choices we make in life.

It is time to empower yourself by taking care of yourself. Every activity—purchase, vacation, manicure, meeting, and hour of overtime—means nothing if you are unhealthy. Affairs, sexual entertainment, seductive songs, pole and belly dancing, doing zumba, and tattoos will not heal you.

It was only through personal responsibility that I, whose parents died when I was young, was able to heal rather than just survive. Yoga heals.

Without healing, we are blind to our infinite potential and innate greatness. We spend money to make ourselves look good rather than invest money to ensure we feel good. We have spent enough time distracting ourselves from what is important; it is time to practice self-care and self-love. It is time to heal.

Healing is a process. If a physical wound is healing, it looks and feels different while it restores itself. The wound goes through a complex process that may take weeks or months. Similarly, when we experience healing at the historical and personal level, we begin by exhaling slowly and deeply, inhaling fresh oxygen, and releasing all the metabolic waste in our bodies.

Àse yoga supports our efforts to be personally responsible and reconnects us to our inheritance of health. The choice is up to us. We are responsible for the way we live. When we change our conditioning, we change our thinking. That is when we open up to this birthright, which reconnects us to our ancient ancestor, Aset.

Aset is the goddess of love, courage, groundedness, and the remover of obstacles. Do you feel unsettled, insecure, and imbalanced? Is there something you want to do but are unable to achieve? Are you sick or struggling? If so, reflect on Aset's challenges as well as her triumphs. Feel her intentions. Feel love resonate through your inhalations and exhalations.

Embrace Aset.

The Power of Aset, an African Deity

I am Aset, one more august and spirit-like than the gods.
—Coffin Texts, spell 148

There is no better way to start activating self-love than to visualize yourself as the goddess Aset, the African goddess of wisdom and love. As you embark on your personal healing journey, picture Aset. Because self-image and self-esteem are closely related to the images you see and the messages you internalize, it is crucial that you see yourself with a right knowledge and recollection. With right knowledge, you do not have to prove that you are beautiful; you just know. Your beauty is revealed to you. You no longer have to pretend. Your lifestyle is evidence that you have a true knowledge of self.

For many of us, our appearances represent a struggle between who we were and what we have become. We pass that struggled down to our daughters. Before the enslavement process, we did not question our beauty but simply experienced it. We did not compare ourselves or our daughters to others. Our inner beauty was connected to our outer beauty. Gradually, things changed. We began to doubt ourselves, as if something was wrong. Our questions changed into feelings that governed the choices we made in our lives. Those feelings have kept us—the people we have become—in conflict with who we really are.

What if what you've been told is false? What if being melanin-endowed, African, and yourself held the secrets of lasting beauty? More importantly, what if someone knew something about you that he or she didn't want you to know?

Aset's energy is intertwined in our lives. Her beauty, wisdom, and love reside in us. I'd known of Aset without really knowing her because over the years she has assumed many names, titles, and appearances. She is the original black Madonna, great mother, healer, protector, divine mother, tender mother, our lady, queen of heaven, guardian of all beings, blessed virgin mother, and mother of God. Do you recognize any of these names? Aset is the divine feminine energy, the primal deity, and shining one.

Aset is often depicted wearing a vulture headdress with a solar disk between a pair of horns, which is sometimes underneath a throne, the symbol of her name. She is also portrayed suckling the infant Hor while seated on a throne. Other images show her wearing the double crowns of north and south Egypt with the feather of Maat or a pair of ram's horns. She may be depicted standing alone with her arms raised to the heavens in a prayer pose.

Growing up Catholic, I knew her as the Blessed Virgin Mother Mary, the mother of Jesus Christ. Her features were European, and she seemed unapproachable. I did not know she was inside of me. I wanted to play her in the nativity school play in elementary school but was told that I was too dark. That didn't stop me from praying to the Blessed Virgin Mother to get me out of something or help me obtain something.

As I retrieved the hidden, treasured images of my existence from my memory, I encountered the goddess Aset. Her story was revealed to me on my journey of self-discovery through the medium of listening. I had grown up without positive images of African women, much less any of an African goddess, and this discovery excited me. In the Kemetic tradition, Aset is the daughter of the earth god Geb and the sky goddess Nut. Her name means "throne, seat, or abode." She is a lunar goddess and is often pictured as the Great Cow. Immediately, I felt a strong kinship and needed to know more about this African goddess imbued with power, beauty, and wisdom.

I often thought love was my downfall but found out later it was a form of power. Aset was the soul mate, partner, lover, and wife of the first king of Egypt, known as Wsr or Asar. According to the story, Wsr's brother, Set, was jealous of Wsr's position and even fell in love with Aset. Set plotted to kill his brother. He asked Wsr to a gathering, which turned into a fight. Set killed his brother, cut him into fourteen pieces, and spread the pieces throughout Egypt. Upset and grief-stricken about the death of her husband, Aset went to find the pieces of his body. Once she found them, she used the energy from her love to put them back together and placed him in a tomb. Then, using divine power, she brought him back to life. Aset turned herself into a hawk and perched on Wsr's erect phallus long enough to take his seed. Miraculously, this beautiful African goddess achieved the impossible through love, life giving, mother force, and compassion.

Love is energy that transforms. It is the force that makes us better human beings. Then Aset gave birth to a son, Hor, who was born during the winter solstice (December 21st). Horus grew up to fight Set and avenge his father's murder. He eventually won the battle. Hor represents the reincarnation of Wsr and higher consciousness.

Over the years, Aset has gone from being black and African to white and European, from being called Aset to being called Isis. Her color and nationality changed, but her essence remained the same. Still, I can't help but ask, if color or nationality didn't matter, then why did she need to change?

This amazing story makes me realize that we have to seek out the truth. We cannot rely on what others have told us. Once we explore, we might find that what we've been told are half-truths. For example, the African woman's image has been distorted and polluted with stories and parables that alter the way we see ourselves. We've assumed the Mammy or Prissy archetype rather than the ones associated with Aset and Hathor. Images shape our reality. When we reconnect with our true images, we act differently.

The story about Wsr and Set is about the proverbial battle that exists within each of us. Our choices can harm others and ourselves or propel us toward wholeness, balance, and love. Some choices leave us fragmented; others connect, unify, and integrate us. How do we connect body, mind, and consciousness? How do we unite our fragmented selves? As I reflected on Wsr's story, it dawned on me that Aset, the feminine deity, shows us how to transform ourselves through love, creativity, compassion, and wisdom.

We carry Aset's spiritual DNA, which can transform not only our lives but also the lives of others. Love is the power behind any transformation and the remover of all obstacles. Aset is love.

What are you struggling with right now? Is something in your life causing conflict and holding you back from your fullest potential? Is it a relationship, fear, unmet needs, health, anger, loneliness, work, depression, family, money, abuse, insecurity, stress, or deprivations experienced in childhood? What makes you jealous, insecure, angry, or unhappy? Those questions can only be answered if you are motionless. In stillness, begin to vibe with Aset's power to heal, transform, and love.

Aset's power is your power. Claim it.

Aset's Energy

Do the following six times. Inhale. Sit in a comfortable position with your legs crossed and spine elongated. Relax your shoulders down your back. Align your ears and head with your shoulders. Place your tongue on the floor of your mouth. Soften your eyes and lips. Look at the picture of Aset. Close your eyes. Visualize the beautiful African goddess Aset in your mind's eye as you draw in a deep loving breath for yourself. Hold for three breaths. Smile inside-out.

Exhale. Slowly lower your arms and hands to toward the earth and relax the tips of your fingers on the ground. Smile. Relax your shoulders, release, and let go. Hold for three breaths. Release any obstacles and challenges.

Inhale. Extend your arms overhead alongside your ears parallel to each other with your palms facing inward while you fully lift your chest. Extend your fingers, stretching them wide toward the sky. Draw in a deep, delicious, heart-centering breath to open yourself to loving experiences. Interlace your fingers over your head and turn your palms up towards the sky. Imagine you're wearing a tall headdress. Pause. Hold for three breaths. Smile inside-out

Exhale. Slowly lower your arms and hands to the floor. Relax the tips of your fingers on the ground. Relax your shoulders, release, and let go. Hold for three breaths. Smile inside-out.

Affirm. *I am powerful, immortal and loving. I am healed, transformed, and whole.*

Tree Pose

The Balancing Power of Àse Yoga

*I am not what happened to me; I am
what I choose to become.*
—Carl Jung

Àse is "conscious energy" Bynum(1999) which manifests as an omnipresence, omniscient, and omnipotent life force. Chukwunyere Kamalu (1997) describes Asé as a vital force whereas Caroline Arewa (1998) links it to pranic energy. This vital and pranic force is within everything you do. The expression of this energy is powerful. Who doesn't want the power to make things happen? When you have power, your life is not based on what happens to you but on how you choose to respond.

The Àse yoga practice is rooted in ancient cosmology, wisdom, and personal experiences. Through this innate vital energy, we can restore wellness, balance, and purpose in your lives. We express Àse by fulfilling our divine purpose, which is not necessarily what we are doing now but our destiny. Fulfilling our destiny is not certain because we have free will. We can do what we want to do, even if it keeps us stuck in the past and affects our ability to live in the present moment.

In practicing Àse yoga, our free will becomes our divine will through a unique healing practice.

At the center of the Àse yoga practice is the belief that we all carry the memory of something in the past that is obstructing our present life and must be released for healing to begin. As I listened to countless stories of grandmothers and grandfathers, mothers and fathers, it became evident that we were passing down the energy of suffering, not the energy of healing. Our history of concentrated trauma and devaluation calls for an energetic healing. Only then can we do the dance of wholeness, unification, and healing.

Àse yoga coaxes this past to the surface so that we can open up space for the regeneration, rejuvenation, and restoration of our energy centers. The experiences of African-American women have been stored in the annals of history as if they didn't happen. Our mothers and mothers' mothers don't talk about them. The time has come for us to celebrate our lives, history, and survival. Àse yoga employs a restorative and receptive practice to encourage the opening of our natural energy centers within our bodies, minds, and spirits. Why restorative? Restorative yoga activates the parasympathetic nervous system, which is responsible for relaxing the body. Being able to relax is essential to our wellbeing. We actively focus on the parasympathetic system, which allows our bodies to return to a balanced state after experiencing stress or trauma.

After enslavement, what did we do to heal? How did we relate to one another? Did we pick up where we left off, or sustain our enslavement behavior? Or did we develop an enslavement syndrome, in which survival behavior became the norm despite its harmful nature. When human beings are enslaved or colonized, they develop maladaptive behaviors in an effort to survive. These behaviors include fear, anxiety, insecurities, phobias, helplessness and coping problems. That proverbial struggle to survive taxes the sympathetic nervous system, creating a "fight or flight" reaction, a physiological response to a threatening experience, during which the pituitary gland releases adrenaline for a massive surge of energy. Our heart rate, breathing, and blood pressure increases. There is maximum blood flow to the limbs. The liver releases sugar, cholesterol, and fatty acids into the blood stream. This struggle didn't end once our ancestors were physically freed. We still harbor psychological reactions from years of subjugation and enslavement that have distorted our wellbeing.

We know trauma can have a lasting effect. It is plausible that the trauma from enslavement still lingers, regardless of how much success or money we have. Knowing that trauma creates a psychobiological imbalance, Àse yoga focuses on releasing and relaxing years of tension within our muscles. In doing so, we release deeply rooted feelings of grief and helplessness and begin to rebalance our vital organs and reignite our life force. Through practice we to stimulate our parasympathetic system, which slows down the heart rate and blood pressure and improves our immune, endocrine, and digestive systems.

We suffer from many stress-related illnesses that can be overcome. Current medical and psychological views have relegated our challenges to a state of permanency and pills. Has a doctor ever told you, "African-Americans tend to have high blood pressure, diabetes, and strokes" and then prescribed a little pill to you? No one ever considered that your blood pressure might be connected to your breathing, which is connected to your current as well as your past experiences, particularly the enslavement experience. Our health and emotional challenges arise from deep within the Atlantic slave trade. Now is the time to let go into the earth, into the waters the chaos, and restore our temples, bodies, minds, and spirits so we can move forward, not as individuals but as a community.

In O Magazine (2007), restorative practices were shown to have the ability to improve blood pressure and decrease the risk of cardiovascular disease and related complications. Our heartbeat speaks to us like the talking drum of conflict. The Àse yoga practice responds with a sequence of heart restorative poses. From this place of self-love, we open up our hearts to forgive others and ourselves unconditionally and let go of anything that is hindering us from love. We touch our hearts, feel the rhythmic beat, and relax our faces with a gentle gaze and inner smile.

Restorative poses are the foundational stones of Àse yoga. When we experience trauma, we tense up. Often that tension stays within our muscles for a lifetime and is handed down to other family members. Through Àse yoga, we learn to break the cycle of stress, tension, and fear through restorative poses, relaxation poses, and an awakening.

Whatever situation you are dealing with—physical, mental, emotional—don't be quick to shrug it off as something connected to what is happening in your life now. Quite possibly, it's the remnants of unreleased or unresolved trauma, disappointment, and stress. Prolonged chaos, pretending to be someone you're not, feeling inferior, being unhappy with who you are, or constantly questioning your existence is stressful.

We all deal with obstacles. A restorative practice will heal our bodies and minds, open our spirits, and eradicate our internal unspoken conflicts. For too long, we have lived in conflict and invisibility. These conflicts will cease only when we connect to love and truth. The moment we embrace our true selves is when our lives will blossom.

When we practice Àse yoga, we respond to traumas, obstacles, and challenges by engaging our breath differently and meditating consistently. Through concentrated restorative poses and energy-balancing movements, we reconnect with our natural beauty and with the insight and wisdom of our ancient ancestors: Aset, Osir, Maat, Tehuti, and Ra. We celebrate our uniqueness. Àse yoga practice is truly an awakening.

Àse yoga is a personalized approach for living a balanced, healthy, and purposeful life. In my research, I've found that we often do not heal because we have not taken the time for healing. We fill our lives with doing other things, such as work, working out, going on vacation. We entertain ourselves by using yoga as an exercise rather than as a powerful healing mechanism. Some think that a yoga class is effective for some people but not for all. Unfortunately, some of us go for the popular trend rather than address the anxiety, low self-esteem, grief, pain, and insecure feelings we harbor. Clearly, your needs are different from someone else's needs because your experiences are different. Àse yoga considers who you are and where you have been so that gradually in your daily practice you become grounded, more centered, and feel less stress while you pursue your divine purpose.

Journaling is part of Àse yoga. Writing down your thoughts, activities, and revelations on a daily basis is encouraged. Throughout my life, I've kept a journal. Journaling helps you clarify your feelings, reflect on the situation, and visually relate to your thoughts. You become a witness, an observer rather than the doer.

Àse yoga opens us to the power of communication or words. We need to express and let go of what has happened during our day, what's on our minds, and what we are feeling. In doing so, Àse yoga engages our thinking patterns and conditioning through conversation and speech. We take time to communicate our obstacles and challenges. Through stories and meditation we transform those obstacles into solutions. This communication prepares us for breath awareness and the ability to be in the present moment.

This aspect of Àse yoga practice focuses on liberating breath, which is more than an instructor saying, "Breathe." In fact, breathing is one of the most important resources of healing. I mirrored a breath of captivity but not liberation. Our breath speaks volumes about where we've been. For instance, my breathing pattern of short inhalations and brief exhalations revealed nervousness, fear, and stress.

We take breathing for granted. However, the quality of our breath responds to how we think and feel. Emphasis is placed on the breath, not as an afterthought or a statement but the heart of the practice. Our breath is the DNA of our experiences. In *The Tao of Natural Breathing: For Health, Well-Being, and Inner Growth*, Dennis Lewis writes, "It is through being 'mindful' of these patterns that we will begin to sense and feel the various psychophysical forces acting on our breath from both the past and present." Our breath tells us where we've been and where we are going. What we know is that breathing is vital to reduce stress, create balance, and restore health. Breathing deeply and exhaling completely relaxes the mind, delivers more oxygen to the bloodstream, and the helps immune system fight infection. We practice Breath Awareness, Three-Part Yogic Breath, Qi Gong Breathing, Nadi-Sodhana, and Ujjayi.

Àse yoga offers a series of neck, leg, and lumbar stretches to create flexibility in the ankles, knees, hips and back, based on the joint-freeing series known as Pavanmuktasana. These practices guide and relax the muscles, increase range of motion, and awaken the energy centers. In doing so, the Àse yoga practice activates our energy centers, regenerates our power centers, and restores our health. Although the focus is on the energy within the spine, Àse yoga works with all the energy radiating throughout our bodies, even in the palms of our hands. As we stretch the arms, hands, and fingertips, we sense an energy flow. The stretches build self-confidence and body awareness as they warm up the body from the soles of the feet to the top of the head. Àse yoga is not a regimen of idle movements. Our movements are about appreciating our bodies while we unite the lower energy with the higher energy. The lower energy is survival, sex, and emotions, while the higher energy is love, wisdom, and divine. A daily practice of opening our major energy centers is encouraged.

Finally, Àse yoga practice is about relating. When open, our energy centers provide a sense of stability, balance, self-love, and empowerment. In relating, our practice focuses on being ourselves and on feeling rather than on performing or moving. By doing so, we experience our own relevancy and a deep sense of wellbeing and healing. Relating is a unique aspect of Àse yoga in that the practice cultivates a sense of fulfillment, openness, and authenticity. Relating is the ability to actively engage in life and access its infinite possibilities. It's not talking; it's communicating. It's not love but loving. It's not trying but doing. It's not wishing but actualizing. In relating, we remove our masks, let down our guard, and become comfortable with ourselves. Most importantly, relating is learning to know ourselves.

An insightful and mindful practice, this yoga style is synchronized with soulful, flowing rhythms and sounds, guided meditation, cascading movements, and lifestyle changes to express Àse. It's not just about the poses; it's about releasing an energetic memory within our bodies, minds, and spirits. That memory affects everything we do and don't do. Within that memory are feelings and emotions that we reframe and release by expressing the power of Àse yoga.

Àse Yoga: Question and Answer

By now, you know, many styles of yoga exist; the aim is the same: to create wholeness, peace, and happiness. Yoga is the uniting of all that we are and can become. Through my studies, interviews with elders, professional experiences, personal revelation, the unveiling of Àse Yoga came to me as a creative way to transform lives.

Àse, a living, breathing, flow of energy, is a powerful vital life force that can bring about amazing results in the physical, mental, and spiritual realms. Expressing Àse is the realization of your purpose and contribution to society. The balancing power of Àse Yoga is designed to access our feelings and thinking, activate the parasympathetic nervous system, and open up the flow of energy for infinites possibilities.

1. What Is Àse Yoga?

Àse yoga is a blend of personal energy, healing asanas, breath awareness, and guided meditation that is designed to stimulate energy, create balance, and facilitate positive relationships with the self and others. Àse yoga is also an energy practice the purpose of which is to access good feelings through healthy living and eating, a balanced lifestyle, and positive communication through the heart. We need energy to fulfill our purpose in life, heal our bodies, and transcend our emotional challenges.

Energy is the force of life that is creative, transforming, and healing. If the question is, *What is energy,* then the answer is, *Everything.* Àse yoga organically moves energy using vibration, rhythm, and movement.

In our lives, we cannot escape the reality of stress and uncertainty. Seventy percent of illness comes from stress. According to a twenty-year study by Kaiser Permanente, 70 to 85 percent of all illnesses that sent patients to doctors were caused by stress. Stress-related illnesses—such as heart disease, stroke, and high blood pressure—are killing us prematurely. However, it's the hidden trauma, the buried suffering within the muscles of our bodies, that we seek to release. Within the Àse yoga practice, stress is viewed as an energetic imbalance. Healing asanas include poses that offset the high levels of activity and mindsets that sustain imbalances and stress. The asanas ground and center us and reawaken love for ourselves and for others.

Àse yoga focuses on the breath of liberation, which emphasizes the exhalation. Many of our past and present experiences have resulted in the release of stress hormones, which foster the "fight or flight" response. This response increases the heart rate and elevates blood pressure. Breathing affects the immune system, suppresses the digestion system, and has a negative impact on mood and motivation. Retraining the way you breathe can reduce the levels of stress hormones in your body, reduce anxiety, calm the nervous system, and activate the relaxation response. How many of us pay attention to our breath? Yet, the breath responds to thoughts, taste, sight, conversations, smell, and everything we do, feel, or touch. Master your breath, and improve your mental and physical wellbeing.

Meditation in Àse yoga centers on the heart chakra, the energy center that opens us to so many emotional challenges and answers. What happened to us during our early years often seals our hearts or distorts the meaning of love. Love is healing. For many of us, heartbreak, disappointment, and toxic relationships have closed our hearts. Our romances, family relationships, and friendships affect our heart. How we perceive those experiences either opens us to embrace loving experiences or closes them off. Guided meditation opens the heart to forgive and love, perceive the experience differently, and move-on lovingly in life. Participants in Àse yoga are encouraged to express love for their loved ones.

Relating is a powerful concept that is concerned with becoming and being you. Difficulties with others and the self are due not to our relationships but in the way you relate. You may often interact with others on a superficial level rather than in authentic ways. Àse yoga infuses the philosophy of relating through conversation because it opens us up to feelings, being authentic, and love. How can you unite with your beloved if you cannot relate to yourself and to others?

2. What Do You Do in Àse Yoga?

Àse yoga is about being rather than doing. Unlike many yoga practices, in which students are constantly doing and feel inept or inflexible, Àse yoga teaches students how to accept themselves. Classes are small and personable so that students can experience inner peace, confidence, and calmness. With an emphasis on breathing, Àse yoga's asanas gently lead every student through an energy-connecting practice of attainable poses, guided meditation, and lifestyle enhancements that open our energy centers for the purpose of transformation. These poses move the body in sequences that encourage students to feel confident and comfortable with their own bodies.

3. Who Can Do Àse Yoga?

Àse yoga is gentle and reflective. It does not put stress or strain on the body, mind, or heart. Often people are afraid or reluctant to attend yoga classes because they feel that their bodies can't do what the media promotes as yoga. Some people even say that they are not flexible or good at doing yoga. Àse yoga is uniquely designed to be where you are and lead you to where you want to go. Finally, Àse yoga incorporates personalization as a key focus in guiding each individual toward self-healing.

Anyone can practice Àse yoga because it is about being and becoming. All of the asanas are inviting, complementary, receptive, and personalized. Àse yoga is an inner experience that expresses itself differently with each student. Never will a student practicing Àse yoga feel inflexible, weak, or imbalanced. Everyone benefits.

Inspiration was drawn from the countless students, who came through the door seeking more than just gymnastic movements and feeling conflicted about yoga. They wanted a practice without judgment, a sense of community and a genuine concern about their life.

4.What Do You Wear to a Àse Yoga Session?

Wear comfortable, loose clothing, preferably 100% cotton to release constriction in your life. Loose clothing allows your body to breathe and lets go of some tightness. Let go of the spandex.

5. What Should I Expect to Get Out of Àse Yoga?

Àse yoga is inspiring, relaxing, and restorative. It gives students what they need through just the right conversation, meditation, asanas, and sound vibration. Students can expect to feel enlivened, deeper sense of relating, restored, inspired, and transformed by the practice and the experience. Focus is on releasing the psosas muscles, opening the heart, feeling the breath and declutterering our mind.

6. What Do I Bring to a Àse Yoga Practice?

Bring your own yoga mat. Owning your own mat is a wise investment and will support your commitment to your practice. Besides, yoga mats carry germs if they are not cleaned on regular basis. Most importantly, make sure you bring an open heart, mind, and spirit.

The Breaths of Liberation

The Lord God formed the man from the dust of
the ground and breathed into his nostrils the breath
of life, and the man became a living being.
—*Genesis 2:7*

We take breathing for granted. Breathing is a gift. Without breath, there is no life. The quality of our breath is crucial to healing. Breath inefficiency can result in a lack of oxygen to our cells and overwhelm our hearts and lungs. Our breath contains life force. When we cultivate this life force, we feel alive, balanced, and energetic.

Our breath says a lot about us and to us. Breathing is sensitive to everything we experience, including our thinking, feelings, and internal and external experiences past and present. Stop for a moment and check-in with your breath. What do you feel? A tightness or difficulty? Do you feel like you're breathing fast or slow, deeply or lightly? When you inhale, does your breath stop at the upper chest around your shoulders or throat area? Are you filling your lungs and expanding your abdomen? Is your chest moving? Is it smooth and consistent or restless and inconsistent? When you exhale is it quick and shallow? Is it complete and releasing?

Simply witness your breath. Don't try to control it. When I observed my breathing pattern, I noticed a lot of anxiety and nervousness when I exhaled. This pattern had to come from somewhere, and I soon discovered where—my early childhood experiences.

As children, our breathing is calibrated with the messages we receive from our parents and caretakers. Children who receive critical, abusive messages inhale quick shallow breaths. Children who receive loving and nonjudgmental messages breathe deeply and exhale completely. So become mindful of what you say and how you speak to your children.

As an adult, I've experienced an almost insurmountable amount of stress, fear, and anxiety. My breathing patterns reflected those same emotions regardless of what was going on. In the end, an unhealthy breathing pattern leads only to unhealthiness. That's why the balancing power of Àse yoga practice re-connects us to our breath. Breathing calms our autonomic nervous system, which includes the sympathetic and parasympathetic or stress and relaxation system. It also focuses our attention, aids us in all our poses and ultimately change our life.

In this section, we will liberate our breath. Give yourself time to experience the following breaths: Breath Connection, Breath Excursion, Three- Part Breathing, Ujjayi Breathing, and Alternate Nostril Breath. Engage in these practices with supervision.

Breath Connection

Life is your ability to breath out every time you breathe in.
—African proverb

S it in a cross leg position or on straight-back chair. Be sure to keep your back softly elongated. Relax your shoulders down your back. Situate your head and ears in alignment with your shoulders. Let your tongue rest at the floor of your mouth. Soften your close lips. Place your hands on your knees with your palms downward. Close your eyes.

Slowly inhale oxygen through your nose, feeling it travel through the nasal passages, into your mouth and down throat into your lungs and expanding your lower ribs. Feel your chest and abdomen expand. Now, feel your rib muscles relax as you release metabolic waste, carbon dioxide, and "old air" for three seconds. Be still, as you continue to breathe in deeply and exhale completely. Connect with the warm and cool air entering and exiting through your nasal passages. Right now, it's just you and breath. If your mind wanders to thoughts, sounds and sensation or if you become distracted, simply bring your attention back to your breath. Our breath is crucial to our wellness, happiness, and prosperity. Practice this exercise for 5 minutes.

Breath Excursion

Merriam-Webster's dictionary defines excursion as a brief pleasure trip. Let's go on an excursion with the breath. Find a quiet place where you will not be disturbed for twenty minutes. Turn off your cell phone, wear loose fitting clothing, preferably 100 percent cotton, and put on relaxing music without vocals. Light incense that is scented with lavender or rose. Place just a drop of essential lavender oil on the tip of your nose.

Lie comfortably on your back or sit up in a chair with your feet on the floor. Inhale. Close your eyes. Feel cool air entering your nose. Soften your face. Notice how your collarbone and the upper part of your chest expand. Placing your hands on either side of your ribs, feel them expand. Place your hands on your abdomen and notice how it rises. Take this time to perform a body scan by drawing your attention to any tension or sensations in your body. Find them, feel them, and release them as you exhale.

Begin to place your attention on your feet, your toes, the soles of your feet, and your heels. Breathe into this area, noticing warm energy flow through your feet up your legs into your knees, pelvis, and tailbone.

While taking this excursion in breathing, rediscover your peace. Draw your breath deeper and slower into your pelvis, sacrum, the bone that forms the back of the pelvis and the tailbone. Pause. Softly say to yourself, "I am feeling good."

Exhale as you slowly release the air from the pelvis to the lungs through the ribcage. Exhale a little deeper. The deeper you exhale, the deeper you relax.

Let the ribs spontaneously come closer together. As you do, your fingertips will come closer together. When the air arrives at the abdomen, draw your navel back toward the spine and release more. As the air flows through the throat and mouth and out through the nose, allow yourself this opportunity to feel good. Pause again,

Take this excursion six times, breathing deeply and exhaling completely. Always remember to feel good. Then resume your normal breathing.

Benefits
• Manages stress
• Relaxation

Three-Part Yogic Breathing

Sit in a comfortable close leg position. Feel your hips, knees, and sitting bones (the bones under the fleshly part of the butt that you sit on) connecting to the earth. Relax your shoulder blades down your back. Elongate your spine. Place head and neck in alignment with your shoulders. Slightly drop your chin toward your chest maintain the upward lift of chest. Place your hands on your knees with your palms down connecting your thumb with your forefinger. Rest your tongue on the floor of your mouth.

Close your eyes. Breathe normally for several cycles. Breathe in fully, rhythmically, and completely. Witness the inhalation and exhalation of your breath without controlling it. Should you become distracted by thoughts, sounds, or sensations, gently bring your attention back to your breath.

Breathe in one third of the way. Inhale deeply through your nose, as you fill your abdomen and lower lungs with air. Expand the belly (which should look like a balloon) with air. Pause for a count of 3.

Draw in more air. Feel the rise to your ribcage. Pause for a count of three.

Breathe in the final third. Breathe into the collarbone causing the area around the heart to expand and rise. Pause for a count of three.

Exhale. Release the air from the belly, drawing the navel back towards the spine, completely reversing the flow. Gently draw the navel back towards your spine to make sure that the belly is empty of air. Now let the ribs slide closer together, release the air from the upper chest, and allow the heart center to sink back down from the rib cage. Pause for a count of six and release. Practice daily.

Benefits
- Releases stress and anxiety
- Grounding and Centering
- Relaxation
- Increases your oxygen supply
- Calms the mind
- Purifies the body

Ujjayi (Throat-Powered Breath)

Assume a seated position or meditation pose with your spine elongated and your head slightly down, as if you are bowing. Place your hands on your knees, palms up, with the tips of your forefingers and thumbs joined in the Jnana Mudra (wisdom seal) and your arms straight. Breathe in deeply and slowly. Focus on your throat.

Inhale slowly, drawing air through your nose, toward the roof of your mouth, partially closing the muscle around the opening of your windpipe (the glottis). You will hear an audible sound, which might resemble a slight hissing sound as you breathe.

Exhale slowly and deeply. Open your mouth and make a soft "ha" sound. This sound is made by slightly restricting the base of the throat (the epiglottis). This constriction makes the sound more audible.

Continue to inhale and exhale slowly and deeply this time with your mouth closed. Make the "ha" sound on the in-breath and out-breath. Maintain your inhalations and exhalations at an even, steady pace. Relax your throat and breath normally.

Practice ujjayi breathing six times. Gradually, your breath will be longer, smoother, and slightly audible.

Benefits
- Calms the nervous system
- Lengthens the breath
- Eliminates phlegm
- Slows your breathing
- Revitalizes the body
- Strengthens the nervous and digestive system
- Releases tension in the solar plexus or abdomen

Alternate Nostril Breathing (One Variation)

Sit comfortably and still, either on a chair or cross-legged on the floor, with a pillow or cushion under your sitting bones supporting the pelvis. In doing so, you should be able to sit erect and protect your back. Close your eyes, relax the body, and breathe normally. Draw your breath to the navel, and let your breathing become smooth and even.

Practice (A): Fold your right index and middle fingers to the palm of the right hand. (This will leave your thumb and baby finger and ring finger out.) Practice (B): You might find it better to place your right index and middle fingers in the center of your forehead between your eyebrows.

If using practice (A), bring your hand to your nose without tipping or turning your head. Lightly place your thumb on the right nostril while the ring finger rests gently on the left nostril. Exhale and than inhale through both nostrils, then gently press the right nostril with your right thumb. Rest the tip of your ring finger and little finger on the side of left nostril. Inhale slowly and deeply through your left nostril to the count of six. Lightly press your left nostril, lift your thumb from the right, and exhale slowly to the count of six. Inhale through the right nostril. Count to six. Gently close your right nostril and exhale through the left nostril to the count to six.

Alternate six times from the right to left nostril, breathing gently and slowly. Lower your hand, and breathe naturally for a minute.

Benefits
- Balances the oxygen and dioxide in your blood
- Regulates the sympathetic and parasympathetic nervous systems
- Creates a sense of groundedness and connectedness
- Counteracts physical and mental tension
- Relaxes the breath

Meditation

*Life is not measured by the number of breaths we take
but by the moments that take our breath away.*

Meditation is a gift from the divine. Meditation relieves you of those experiences that weigh you down while clothing you in the riches of the universe and escorting you to a place of balance and happiness. Meditation is a primary aspect of yoga and must become a part of your daily routine. You wouldn't forget to brush your teeth, comb your hair, or eat? Well, now you should include meditation on your must-do list.

To meditate is to heal. Enduring and surviving is not enough; we must begin to heal. When we meditate, we see ourselves differently. We can properly bury our past suffering to make space for our new life. Furthermore, meditation transforms and promotes the much-needed balance in our life.

Through meditation you surrender to a higher consciousness. Meditation is not simply closing your eyes. It is a process of emptying the mind and quieting the spirit. You can start with breath awareness meditation or guided meditation. To benefit from meditation, you must practice it on a regular basis.

Take a few minutes to mediate each day. Begin by meditating daily for ten minutes and increase to twenty minutes after twenty-one days. Try to meditate in the morning before you rush out of the house or get busy. The following is a list of ways to prepare for meditation:

- Sit down in a comfortable cross-legged position or in lotus pose
- Slow down
- Turn off all of your electronic devices, i.e., cell phones, television, and music
- Close your eyes and elongate your spine
- Don't eat two hours before you meditate
- Meditate alone in a quiet room lit by candles
- Do some light exercises, such as qi gong or structural yoga, before meditating
- Chant a word of power (a mantra or *hekau*) for a few minutes to set up positive vibrations in the mind: *So Hum, Ham'sa* (I am that—awareness). *Nuk sah em ba-f* (I am spirit, with my soul). *Un-na uat neb am pet am ta* (The power is within me to open all doors in heaven and earth)

Guided Meditation

To prepare, light your favorite incense to set the mood. I prefer lavender and sandalwood. Play meditative music softly in the background.

Something terrible happened in our lives, as individuals and as a collective. Although our story has been mistakenly told as a slave story, nothing could be further from the truth. It's a story of survival and must become one of enlightenment. In doing so, we will realize that our lives can be transformed by these experiences. We can stop the cycle of victimization, helplessness, ignorance, avoidance, shame, anger, and conflict.

Our families, our friends, and our communities call out for healing.

That healing begins with us. We must be the change that we want in others. It starts with feeling grounded to our spiritual mother, loving ourselves, and transforming into good people, healthy parents, and wise elders. We must turn off the nonsense that disturbs our senses, insults our intelligence, and corrupts our children. Say no to the over sexualization of our daughters, the low expectations of our sons, and the mis-education of all of us. Say no to the music, sports, and entertainment that diminish our vital energy and hasten our breath.

We all have a story to tell as to why we are the way we are. We have a story about why we are angry or happy, miserable or fulfilled, aggressive or peaceful, educated or mis-educated, poor or prosperous. Whether that story becomes a lesson learned or an ongoing drama of suffering is up to us. Life may or may not have given us what we wanted, but life has given us a choice. Every person we've met, every suffering we've endured, and every joy we've embraced has been life giving us opportunities, choices, and support. Understand that life and wisdom will follow. And only though wisdom will transformation occur.

Our ancestors understood primeval chaos and suffering, life force and power. We commit acts of harm to others and ourselves when we choose chronic chaos instead of the life force. Now is the time to let go of all wrongs and disappointments that we carry. It's time to live. If we look at our lives deeply enough, we can access the life force that brings light to our inner enlightenment.

Our ancestors and foremothers were part of complicated generations. This generations experienced discrimination, Jim Crow, desegregation, The Great Depression, lynching, and war. They were separated from their families and enslaved. Even after emancipation they had to fight for rights that we take for granted.

Born out of unique situations and circumstances, we have inside of us the power through ourselves, our relationships, and our creations to breathe love, forgiveness, and healing into the world. Healing is power. It is sacred. If we seek healing, then we change more than ourselves, a generation. To accept unhappiness, misery, and fear is to give up. Too much have been done for us; it's time that we do for ourselves.

Let these words penetrate your mind.

Practice the following three times. As you inhale deeply, count quietly to two and release to the count of four. Focus your mind on your breath. Observe the inflow and outflow of your breath. If your mind is distracted by thoughts, sounds, or sensations in your body, focus and gently return your attention to your breath. Gently, close your eyes, release any tension, aches and pains in your body into the earth, and focus on your rhythm of your breath. Soften your face. Relax your jaw. Silently repeat your personal mantra.

Allow your breath to flow in and out slowly, comfortably, and naturally for 20 minutes. Be patient. Be steadfast. Be forgiving. Plant the seeds to love yourself, forgive yourself and others, and invest in healing.

Benefits
- Changes mental and physical health for the better
- Improves quality of life
- Decreases addictions, at-risk behaviors, and the effects of stress

Feeling Good: Chakra Tuning

How do you feel right now? Is it the same way you've felt for the last twenty or more years? Are you stuck in a rut? Did the end of a relationship leave you feeling out of balance? Did you lose your job, fail a test, or move? Are you trying to achieve something but have not yet done it? Are you feeling sick or afraid? What are you doing or not doing? Where are you? What illnesses are you battling?

Don't be so hard on yourself. What's happening in your life at this moment has more with your inner structure than your external experiences. Your inner physiology is the executor of everything that happens in your life. Although you may not see it, your body is home to subtle energy that fuels our activities and choices in life.

We understand our physical body, what we look like, and our internal organs; however, we rarely discuss the subtle anatomy. What happens to us and for us flows deeply into our being, causing us to respond one way or another. Beyond the surface exists an anatomy that cannot be seen with the eyes. However, it can be experienced through the breath, meditation, and connecting with a deeper essence of ourselves. In fact, this subtle energetic functioning, which includes energy centers, breath, and Ase, affects the physical body and has the ability to bring wellness, prosperity, and liberation into existence. Anything we want to accomplish requires energy. Through *The Art of Feeling Good*, we activate this astonishing flow of natural energy.

Unfortunately, we live in a society that emphasizes the seen while ignoring the unseen. Just because we can't see it doesn't mean it isn't happening. How we feel, what we do, and how we communicate as well as our self-image, choices, and whether we are at peace corresponds to our powerful energy fields. Our physical or mental ailments have corresponding energy equivalences. When we experience a physical ailment, it is often caused by an imbalance that exists on an energy level.

When we only address the physical, we wrongly assume that we are only composed of a physical body: hair, nails, clothes, skin, bones and muscles. In truth, we exist on a deeper energetic or electromagnetic level. For example, when the surgeon removed the diseased portion of my body to sustain my life, intuitively I knew more work needed to be done. So I opened my energy centers to fully revitalize my life force in certain areas, such as around my heart.

The energy centers I am referring to are known as chakras. Have you heard of them? If not, I invite you to get to know them. Each chakra has its own meaning, function, location, color, element, deity, vibration, physical and psychological correspondent, rhythm sound, and other attributes. We host hundreds of energy centers throughout our bodies, extending into our fingertips.

For now, we will explore the seven major energy centers known as chakras: five along the spinal column, one in the forehead, and the other above the skull. The word "chakra" means wheel. These seven major energy centers rotate rapidly and rhythmically at specific juncture points. They allow energy to flow freely from the universal energy field into the body at seven separate locations.

These energy centers rely on sensory and emotional stimulation during the waking state, which are converted into the life force (or *prana*, chi, or Àse) to keep the subtle and physical body balanced. Sensory stimulation includes music, smells, television shows, food, etc. Emotional stimulation includes early childhood experiences, enslavement, grief, stress, chaotic parenting, poverty, feelings of liberation, peace, forgiveness, and contentment. Depending on the stimulation, the chakras become open and functional or blocked and sluggish. When the chakras are open, energized, and balanced, we feel alive and at peace. In contrast, when we are depressed, angry, unmotivated, and insecure our energy flow is weakened. The good news is that we can activate the energy to ensure we feel good.

Rarely do people say their chakras are not functioning or that they have a sluggish chakra. You might hear someone say they have a stomachache, but you won't hear them say they are afraid or worried. The stomachache, fears, and worries are connected. What we do for the stomachache is take a pill, but what do we do to combat the fear? We might not need to take the pill if we open the energy in the corresponding chakra. What do we do about lack of motivation or self-love? What do we do about low self-esteem? And what do we do about anger, disappointment, abuse, and heartbreak?

Chakras are the elixir within our lives. Depending on their vitality, we will either continue to be sick, poor, insecure, tired, cold, and foolish or happy, prosperous, and healthy. What's happening in our lives, what we do for living, and the relationships we attract relate to the healthiness of our chakras or energy centers.

Most of us operate at a level where our chakra energy is sluggish or neglected and thus in need of consistent attention. We suffer not so much from clinical depression but from situational depression. We are not bipolar but suffer from an imbalance. We don't have a lack of talent but a lack of energy. We don't have a lack of information but a lack of self-knowledge. Because of conditions, challenges, and obstacles in our everyday lives we have less energy to convert to *prana*, chi, or Àse. As a result, we don't follow through on our intentions. We engage in the wrong relationships. We fail to keep our word. We're angry. We procrastinate. We're tired and unmotivated. We experience a host of stress-induced diseases.

Parts of the past, personal challenges, and early childhood disturbances necessitate chakra healing. Our enslavement experiences have affected current energy patterns and require that we take the time to heal. From the 1400s to the present, our energy has been repeatedly challenged, which has resulted in the adoption of less-than-optimal ways of thinking and acting. As women, we have settled too often for the illusion of love rather than the reality.

Your thoughts convince you to do things that deactivate your energy. If you think a certain way long enough, your thoughts become your reality, which predisposes helplessness, fear, and energy disturbances. As such, you gravitate toward relationships out of fear, not self-love.

For too many years, we were physical, financially, and mentally disempowered. Even though we are now physically free, the patterns of those imprinted behaviors still exist. This is not an excuse but an explanation. Until we take personal responsibility for healing, our energy centers will continue to function inefficiently. Once we realize that we have the potential to become enlightened, be happy, and feel good, will we choose to do so?

A consistent practice of chakra tuning unblocks the energy channels and encourages an optimal level of life force to promote vital health and energy and a sense of wholeness and purpose in our lives. We will feel amazing. We've endured the enslavement process, personal suffering, unthinkable atrocities, and discrimination; why not embrace a journey toward wholeness and peace?

Our Seven Major Energy Centers

Touch the Earth, Feel Connected, Come Home

Mūladhara, the root chakra, is located at the base of the spine or tailbone. In women, it sits between the vagina and uterus. The goddess Kundalini resides there as a coiled snake wrapped three-and-a-half-times around. We want to wake her up because her awakening connects us to Mother Earth, love, self-responsibility, and body appreciation. Our root, or foundational energy, is about fulfilling our physical survival needs and basic human potentiality. Essentially, the root energy grounds and centers us. Here we feel connected to our bodies. We feel stable and secure. We are full of energy, healthy, and unattached. No longer are we as Ralph Ellison said, "invisible ... because people refuse to see [us]." We become visible because we have the courage and confidence to see ourselves.

Many of us experienced feelings of uprootedness during early childhood. For me, the death of my mother and the displacement that followed de-stabilized my innate root energy. At the time, I didn't realize that this experience would result in insecurity, financial problems, stagnation, and poor choices in relationships, chronic constipation, and underachievement. The more I learned, the more it became apparent that African Americans carry a complex set of emotions that were transmitted through the enslavement process. In addition to my mother's death, the unspoken circumstances of her life as an African-American woman also affected me. Both of these experiences created chronic imbalances in my life that affected my health and happiness.

In my clinical practice, I often heard stories from women who lacked healthy mothering because their biological mothers were drug addicts, in toxic relationships, alcoholics, mentally unstable, preoccupied with other things in life, or deceased. As adults, these women still longed for what they didn't receive as children. They still felt disappointment, a void, and confusion. As little girls, they had to take care of younger siblings, were sexually abused, or were verbally berated by their mothers. Their lack of emotional connection with a positive mother figure created a longing in them that can only be fulfilled through healing. As parents, they sometimes mimic what they experienced as children or overcompensate by giving their children what they didn't receive, which creates an imbalance within the children.

Take a moment to reflect on your relationship with your mother. What do you feel? Is it sadness, confusion, bitterness, emotional abandonment, resoluteness, hunger, or homelessness? Or do you feel happiness, love, inspiration, and gratitude?

Over the course of our history, African-American women were constantly uprooted and moved from one plantation to another. They had no control of their bodies. Imagine being captured and taken from your home and family. Certainly, such actions affected the women's neural pathways and those of their children, grandchildren, and other descendants. Earlier conditioning and cultural trauma blocked the flow of energy in our root chakra, resulting in habits and patterns that have had a negative impact on our health, minds, and spirits.

Somewhere along the way, we've become ashamed of our experiences and stopped dealing with them. Then a variety of challenges—anxiety or panic attacks, clinging to unhealthy relationships, restlessness, preoccupation with hair or looks, overconsumption, subordination to needs of others, neglecting one's own body, and a lack of responsibility about one's own life—become reminders of reality. Until we acknowledge that the source of our problems lies not only in the present but also in the past, we will continue to deal only with the symptoms.

Enslavement compromised our sense of stability and security and our connection to the earth. It also led to a host of long-lasting experiences that upset the free flowing energy of the root. We've made accomplishments despite these experiences, not because of them. However, our achievements sometimes come at price.

When you were a child, what messages did you hear about yourself as an African-American female? What kind of relationship did you have with your mother? Were you hungry? Did you wear second-hand clothing? How often did you move? How many evictions or car repossessions did you endure? Are you fulfilling or sabotaging your potential? Has your mother transitioned? What messages did you receive as child about your life goals? Were you told to find a job that would make you a lot of money or one that would make you happy? Did you hear a lot of complaints about money? Were you a foster child or an adoptee? Were you abused or abandoned? Did you grow up in household that was preoccupied with designer brands? Do you engage in self-destructive behaviors by overeating or not eating enough?

We'd all like to think that none of this matters; yet the quality of our lives and our children's lives depend on the vitality of our root chakra. When I was a child, I didn't hear or see positive message about African-American women.

However, as I grew up, I encountered wonderful mother figures that nurtured me.

Blockage

If you feel stressed, overly materialistic, overwhelmed, stuck in rut, fearful, and constricted, it may be a root block. When this occurs, you may want to activate a fight-or-flight response because your body feels under attack. Your adrenal glands, which sit on each of the kidneys, produce adrenaline (also known as epinephrine), which regulates the heart rate and circulatory system. It prepares the body to either fight the foe or flee from danger.

When you feel stressed, fearful, and anxious, your thoughts can produce too much adrenaline. This causes a number of physical symptoms, such as a change in heart rate, tightness in the chest, breathing difficulties, and a feeling of being out-of-control. You may also experience paranoia and hallucinations, headaches, digestive problems, insomnia, and fatigue. Other problems include constipation, knee problems, back pain, depression, and weight concerns. These are all root imbalances. Other root imbalances relate to issues such as finding or keeping a job, body distortion, trouble paying bills, toxic relationships, worry, fixating on becoming rich, hoarding, clinging behaviors, fear, nervousness, and homelessness.

Do any of these symptoms sound familiar? I believe many of us suffer from varying degrees of insufficient energy flowing through our root chakra, even those who make a lot of money. The cars we drive, the size of our houses, the vacations we take, and our professional status cannot substitute for a lack of grounding. If we do absolutely nothing, then our root stays blocked or sluggish and eventually physical and emotional illness occurs. Unfortunately, people don't seek help until after the subtle has manifested and a doctor has diagnosed a medical problem.

Unlock the Energy

Let go of the hustles, the I-hate-my-job attitude, ego, frustration, situational depression, tiredness, family issues, materialism, indecisiveness, the just-being-over-broke syndrome, and the anxieties about being successful. Let go of the insecurities, instabilities, dependencies, and physical hang-ups. Open the root chakra, also known as the foundation, so that you feel stable and secure, grounded and centered. Unblock or remove the debris from the root to experience groundedness. That debris includes wrong knowledge, distorted thoughts, habits and patterns of behavior that sustain internalized fear, insecurities, and instabilities in the face of challenges.

Perfect Journey

Lie down on your back with your arms resting comfortably by your side. If you wish, put a blanket underneath your head. Extend your legs and separate them a little. Face your palms upward. Close your eyes. Take a deep breath in through your nose and slowly exhale as you release enslavement experiences, feelings of neediness, your present challenges, fears, insecurities, and anxieties. Enslavement experiences include fear, powerlessness, envy, anxiety, panic, fatigue, subjugation, alienation, and conflict. Just let it all go. Let your breath flow in and out.

Become comfortable as you move the energy, the life force, from your feet up your legs into your pelvis and your sacrum. (The sacrum, which is known as the sacred bone, is a large, triangular bone at the base of the spine or below the lumbar spine.) The tailbone attaches to the bottom of the sacrum. Our sacrum carries the weight of the body to the pelvic girdle.

Draw your breath to the base of your spinal cord or root chakra. Visualize the base of your spine glowing bright red. Feel the root chakra channeling your energy of security, wholeness, stability, and balance. Connect with your breath.

Breathe slowly and deeply though your nose. Release your frown, soften your face, and let go of your thoughts. Focus on your breath. Relax your body as you connect with your foremothers and grandmothers. Connect with your ancestors and Mother Earth.

Exhale as long as you can. Then inhale deeply, visualizing the goddess Aset removing all of your obstacles. Allow yourself this opportunity to release your fears, victimhood, attitudes, and any feelings of insecurity or instability. Release into the earth anything that no longer serves you. Connect with Àse, your life force and your inner power.

Visualize your body as a temple of light. Turn on the light inside your body and sense the electromagnetic energy pulsating at the base of your spine. Appreciate your body through healthy living and healthy eating.

Feel your life force awakening. Feel Kundalini becoming aroused with each inhalation and exhalation. Know that you belong here and are protected. No matter what you experienced before your birth, as a child, or as an adult, the universal omnipresence, the divine Mother Earth supports you. Into the earth, surrender thoughts of limitations, motherlessness, negativity, obstacles, and residual enslavement mindsets.

Inhale freedom. Exhale enslavement. Breathe deeply and slowly, six times, in and out. Place a tiger's eye crystal over your root chakra. This will support your journey toward groundedness and centeredness. Release tension and calm your mind. You belong here. Celebrate your earth day. Be still with your in-body experience for fifteen minutes. Welcome yourself home.

To further open up your root energy, practice the following sequence. Close your eyes. Laying on your back with your face upward, gently pull your knees toward your chest. Breathe in, holding your knees over your hip, feeling your belly expand. Observe your lower back rising slightly off the floor.

Breath out pull you knees back toward your chest feeling your thighs press gently into your lower belly, and observe your lower back press into the floor. Repeat the movement six times. Alternate pulling in and relaxing.

Root Chakra

- Function: physical survival, identity, groundedness, body awareness
- Location: Between genitals and anus or uterus
- Endocrine gland: adrenal
- Color: red
- Essential oils: sandalwood, patchouli
- Crystal: tiger's eye
- Deity: Aset
- Element: earth
- Yoga pose: Energy Opening Pose and Bridge Pose
- Breath: breath awareness
- Meditation to the earth
- Journaling
- Imbalances: security, dependence, low self-esteem, fear, materialism, and self-destructive behavior

The Greatest Love of All Resides Inside You

Svadisthana, the sacral (sex) chakra, is located in the lower abdomen between the navel and genitals. It corresponds to the testes or the ovaries that produce the various sex hormones involved in the reproductive cycle. The sacral chakra is concerned with basic emotional needs, pleasure, self-love, and relationships, as well as violence, addictions, and lack of self-confidence. It is the center of sexuality, emotions, and creativity—the headquarters of all our creative energy.

Nowadays, much emphasis is placed on the sacral chakra as a sex act independent of the other energy centers. Sex is natural, and, yes, it sells. However, it's not the tightness or shortness of your clothes that makes you sexy or erotica that makes you seductive; it's the sacral or sacred energy vibrating within. This energy is more about sensuality than sex. Sex is definitely a reality in our lives, but our sense of self-worth is more important.

How do we learn to love ourselves when we place so much emphasis on finding someone to love us? How can we love another person when we haven't learned to love ourselves? We spend our time beginning and ending relationships with others when the problem is not the other person; it's a lack of self-love. How can we love ourselves when sex is performed, not enjoyed? Being sexy is akin to saying, *I want to be wanted or desired by others*. But how can we want something from others that we have not given ourselves. Loving-who-we-are is fundamental to this energy. To do that, we must ask the question "Who am I?"

Historically, African-American women have been depicted as Jezebels or Mammy's. I grew up around African-American women who were depicted as unattractive. What child wants to resemble that image? At times, we're depicted as oversexed; at other times, as inhibited. Some of us have opted to act out the stereotype without understanding how to connect with our sensuality.

If we reflect on our history, we find documented accounts of rape, abuse, molestation, and unimaginable demands placed on our bodies to breed. According to the "Black Women's Health Imperative," 40 percent of black women have experienced some form of sexual assault or abuse. It's not uncommon for an African-American female to share in therapeutic setting that they were sexually abused but never spoke about it. Sexual abuse is too often the dirty little secret that claims numerous victims. We act out because of it but don't seek healing to reclaim our lives. We can't control what happen to us, we can only choose to respond in a way that doesn't continue to harm us.

Although African-Americans make up about 13 percent of the US population, AIDS is the primary killer of African-Americans ages nineteen to forty-four. The mortality rate is ten times higher for black Americans than for whites. The most recent statistics from the Centers for Disease Control indicate that 45 percent of all new cases of HIV infection are among African Americans. We change these numbers by changing ourselves.

When we love ourselves, we make healthier choices. How many of you have engaged in behaviors that exposed you to sexually transmitted diseases, allowed someone to disrespect you, or led you to participate in an adulterous affair or a one-night stand in the pursuit of pleasure? We assume the role of victim when we choose inappropriate sexual partners. We tell ourselves that what we don't know won't hurt us. When we do, we fail to take personal responsibility for our sexual health. Our desire to be wanted is greater than our ability to love ourselves.

Blockage

When we feel overly emotional, manipulative, and sexual addictive, guilty for no reason, hypercritical, overly sensitive, and frigid or impotent, it means the energy in the sacral charka is congested.

We reenact the enslavement mentality in our intimate relationships, because we lack love and respect for ourselves. We cannot escape the fact that the enslavement process conditioned us as breeders, rather than lovers. We cannot escape that to feel love; to open oneself to intimacy, to express oneself freely was not possible for more than four hundred years within the African-American community. As such, some of us develop a dysfunctional way of relating sexually to one another so that the energy flows downward toward sex rather than upward toward love. Consider this: whatever choices we make in life, monogamy, serial monogamy, secular affairs, group marriage, polygamy, or polyandry must come from self-love rather than fear or hardship.

Unlock the Energy

To activate this energy we need to trust and love ourselves. What is the first word that comes to your mind regarding sex? Pregnancy or Pleasure? Are you open to experiencing sex as a creative energy rather than sex on demand or for procreation? Do you perform sex just to get it over with? What are your fantasies? Do you see sex as a bargaining chip, i.e.., *If I give sex, I'll get a Gucci bag, a vacation, a dinner, etc.*? Have you stop being sexual? Do your respect yourself? What are you "trying" to create? Why have you not done so? This wonderful chakra transforms the finite into the infinite. It unlocks your limitless energy.

Perfect Journey

If we stay the course, our energy moves from the root to the sacral center. Lie on the floor. Extend your legs straight out. Draw your shoulders away from your neck. Be still. Bend your knees and pull your feet up toward your genitals. Allow your knees to fall out to the sides, stretching the insides of your thighs. Focus on your lower back and gently relax into the floor. Shift your focus to your pelvis and press your tailbone into the floor, engaging your pelvis and releasing your psoas muscles. (Our psoas muscles connect our trunk and legs and enable us to flex our thigh and hips. They also hold deep emotional tension.) Releasing our psoas muscles is critical to our healing and immune system. Now close your eyes, and breathe into your pelvis. Breathe into your sexual organs. Your whole body will relax. Release any tension in your hips.

Inhale deeply and visualize a pleasurable experience. Draw your breath into your pelvis. Visualize the color orange. Exhale, letting go of anything that blocks your creativity, emotions, and sexuality. Let go of years of messages and programming that have inhibited your ability to feel pleasure and encouraged frigidity. Let go of any unhealthy relationships.

Begin to love and express yourself sensually. Connect with the curves in your body. Respect the journey it has been on. Whether due to breast cancer, surgery, pregnancy, or growing older, your body has changed. See it as perfect and beautiful.

With a Carnelian crystal on your sacrum to regulate your emotional self, breathe deeply six times, in and out. Reflect on your personal creations. See yourself as authentic love.

Feel your worthiness. Repeat, "I love myself" five times, inhaling and exhaling. Connect with the beautiful water goddess, Yemoja. Inhale her beauty, creativity, and sensuality. Feel her presence.

Sacral Chakra

- Function: creativity, emotion, sexuality, self-esteem
- Location: lower abdomen between the navel and genitals
- Endocrine: gonads, ovaries, testes
- Color: orange
- Essential oils: orange essential oil
- Crystal: Carnelian
- Deity: Yemoja
- Element: water
- Yoga pose: Bound Angle and Pelvic Tilt
- Breath: Ujjayi
- Meditation to the water
- Journaling
- Imbalances: manipulation, sexually addiction, womanizing, emotional insensitivity, frigidness, impotency, jealousy, lack of self-confidence, and lower back pain

You've Got the Power

Manipura, or solar plexus chakra energy, is located at the base of the ribcage. It ignites our metabolism and digestive system. The solar plexus is governed by fire and power. This is the chakra of *making things happen*. Personal power, transformation, fears of rejection, procrastination, anxiety, judgment, and anger arise in this center. As we experience self-acceptance and self-respect, we cultivate our personal power for overcoming and facing challenges. When we are alone and not pretending to be someone else, how do we really feel about ourselves? Those internal, unspoken feelings dictate what we do in life. With this energy, we can choose to be a warrior or a victim, an orphan or the beloved. The question that arises is, *What is my purpose?*

Blockage

What are you doing or not doing with your life? Are you tired? Do you feel like you don't have any energy? Are you procrastinating? What obstacles or challenges do you face? We go only as far as our thoughts will allow. If we think something isn't possible, we won't do anything to make it happen. What we tell ourselves either limits or empowers us. Far too often, the messages we received as children have more to do with what we can't do than what we can do. Messages of submissiveness and docility have been programmed inside us.

As a result, we've become workaholics and aloof in our relationships with others. Money rather than service to others has become our sole goal. Although we may look successful, we are angry, controlling, judgmental, and downright mean to others. We see ourselves as efficient; actually, we're afraid. How many ideas, inventions, jobs, projects, and incomplete manuscripts have you accumulated? Are you working in a profession that you don't enjoy? If so, you have not connected to your personal power. You've been off the path too long. Get back on the path and continue your journey, this time feeling empowered. What you have learned from your challenges can only make you stronger. Go forth, and make it happen.

Lynching and torture transmits a feeling of powerlessness through the generations. According to Robert Zangrando in "About Lynching," more than three thousand African-American men were lynched in the United States between 1882 and 1968. In "Beautiful, also, Are the Souls of My Black Sisters," Sheryl Gay Stolberg notes that during the same period an untold number of African-American women were lynched, including Laura Nelson, Jennie Steers, and Maggie and Alma Howze. Even though that physical reality no longer exists, the psychological response endures. We must let go of the all the negative thoughts and actions that accompanied the pain of our ancestors. We must let go of all of the thoughts that have been disempowering us. Our reality defines our response.

Unlock the Energy

Light that inner fire. Activate your inner solar system. Let go of the psychological shackles. Understand that no one can give you freedom. Feel freedom and energy vibrating in your solar plexus. Take the creations you have cultivated in your sacral chakra and transform them into a reality.

Empower yourself. Transform your anger, your attitude, and your subservience into unlimited potential. Banish words and thoughts that disable you. Awaken those dormant dreams by breathing life into them. Stop settling. You were born to fulfill a purpose.

Perfect Journey

Lie down on your back with your arms resting by your sides. Let your palms face up. Take a deep breath in, and slowly exhale. Let your breath flow easily in and out as you move your breath to your navel area and your solar plexus. Close your eyes. Release your frown, soften your face, and free your mind.

Now, exhale as long as you can. Then inhale spontaneously, visualizing Ra, the sun god, and embrace divine light, nature's solar power. When exhaling, allow yourself the opportunity to release fear and any thoughts that block your vision and creativity. Inhale the warrior power to overcome life's challenges. Exhale any person or situation you have given your personal power to. Say their names and release them.

Breathe deeply six times, in and out. Place your sunstone crystal over your solar plexus chakra to support your journey toward transformation and personal power. Inhale. Silently say to yourself, "I've got the power." Again, exhale any person or situation you have given your power to, even if it's your thoughts. Release tension and calm your mind. Exhale a little deeper into your solar plexus. Visualize the color yellow to help activate your solar energy.

Warrior Pose
Stand with your feet parallel. Adjust your feet so that your right foot faces twelve o'clock and your left foot points toward ten o'clock. Exhale, separate your legs about 5 feet apart. Inhale as you raise your arms above your head and your palms face one another. Extend your fingers, keeping them together except for the thumbs. Keep them open. Exhale as

you turn your torso, shoulders and arm to face your right foot. Bend your right knee until your shins form a perpendicular line with the floor. Make sure your back leg is straight, and weight balanced evenly. Inhale, adjusting your torso so that your pelvis and shoulders squarely face forward. Remain steady in the pose for at least six slow breaths. Inhale as you straighten your knee, returning to center position. Repeat on the opposite side.

Solar Plexus Chakra

- Function: vitality, metabolism, digestive system, feelings, inner power
- Location: base of the sternum
- Endocrine gland: pancreas
- Color: yellow
- Essential oil: geranium
- Crystals: sunstone, yellow citrine
- Deity: Ra
- Element: fire
- Yoga pose: Warrior Pose
- Breath: victorious breath
- Meditation on inner power and light
- Journaling
- Imbalances: anger, being judgmental, controlling, self-consciousness, uncertainty, inability to make decisions, insecurity, depression, violence, hyperactivity, hypoactivity, excess weight, stomach ailments

It's Time for Love, So Let's Get Ready

A nahata (the heart chakra) is located in the center of the chest, right next to your heart. Place your right hand on your chest, a little to the left of the center of your body. Feel your heartbeat in the middle of your chest. This energy speaks to a smorgasbord of emotions, such as peace, compassion, tenderness, forgiveness, loving energy, unconditional love, equilibrium, and well-being. Physically, the heart chakra presides over circulation; emotionally, it regulates unconditional love for self and others.

Blockage

We carry weight that blocks our ability to love. Relationships with our parents or caretakers, friendships, and romances can make the energy in this chakra quite challenging. Sometimes we are with our partners out of fear rather than love. That fear comes from what we didn't receive earlier in life. We try to compensate. Unfortunately, we do ourselves a disservice because we cannot grow when our hearts are closed.

Telling or showing love for someone else without requiring it to be reciprocated is difficult. To love is to be vulnerable, so it is difficult to form loving relationships. Love is not a possession. You cannot possess another person. No one belongs to you or is yours. Only through the healing power of love will we realize this fact.

When our relationships are possessive, manipulative, emotionally abusive, oppressive, clinging, and based on insecurity and excessive neediness, the heart energy is congested. Behaviors and thoughts that signal that something is wrong with the heart chakra, include hiring private detectives, reading the cell phone text of your spouse or significant other, mistrust, and a preoccupation with sex. To use another person for sex, money, or reproductive reasons contaminates the heart's energy. We can't love because we fear rejection. Deep down we feel unworthy because of our unmet needs. We try to compensate for these traits through materialism and inappropriate sexual behaviors.

Unlock the Energy

Feel your heartbeat as it opens to feelings of security, stability, self-love, empowerment, transformation, the power to love unconditionally, and the practice of compassion and forgiveness. Begin to blossom. Let's begin. Add on what you feel needs to be forgiven:

- Forgive the mother who was not physically or emotionally present in your life.
- Forgive the father who abandoned you.
- Forgive the sister who hurt you.
- Forgive the brother who chooses to be a drug addict.
- Forgive the friend who lied to you.
- Forgive the child who didn't achieve what you wanted him to achieve.
- Forgive the boyfriend who cheated on you.
- Forgive the husband who left you.
- Forgive your coworkers who deceived you.
- Forgive the supervisor who terminated you.
- Forgive yourself.

Perfect Journey

Sit in a chair with your feet on the floor. Close your eyes. Place your hands on your heart, and feel your heartbeat. Breathe deeply and slowly. Soften your face and smile. Inhale deeply, letting your abdomen expand and exhale slowly; then let it contract. Do this six times.

Now draw your breath into your heart, filling it up with all the good things that have happened to you. Exhale any experiences that block your ability to feel, express, and be love. It's time to open up your heart.

Sphinx Pose
Lie face down on the floor. Bring your hands directly under your shoulders. Keep both elbows on the ground and let your forehead touch the floor. Now slowly raise your head, shoulders, and chest. Keep your feet together on the floor. Continue to lift up into a sphinx-like posture. Lengthen your spine, and breathe deeply. As you open your heart, allow it to fill with love and wisdom. Feel the embodiment of power and enlightment.

Cobra Pose
Lie on your stomach with your head or chin on the floor. Place your arms by your sides with your palms facing down and your fingertips in line with your breastbone. Keep your elbows pointed upward; then pull your shoulders back and down. Keep your legs together, press the tops of your feet into the earth, lengthen your tailbone toward your heels, and draw your lower abdominal muscles in toward your spine.

Breathe in as you raise your head and chest, pulling upward on your lower back and lifting your upper back away from the floor. Lower your shoulders away from your ears as you lift your chest. Keep your neck elongated as you look straight ahead.

Exhale as you bend your back, keeping your arms close to your body. Length your spinal column for six breaths. Breathe smoothly. Inhale as you lengthen your chest.

Slowly lower your head back on the floor and turn on your back.

Breathe deeply. Bend your knee, and draw them into your chest. Gently rock from side to side. Exhale as long as you can. Then inhale deeply, visualizing the goddess Maat. Let go of any grudges and behaviors that hinder you. Let go of past relationships that no longer serve you, including toxic relationships, expectations of others, and any heartbreak. Make space for right relationships and new life. Visualize the color emerald green at your heart center. As you forgive yourself and others, place the rose quartz on your heart chakra to stimulate self-love and unconditional love for others.

Heart Chakra

- Function: Unconditional love, self-acceptance, transformation
- Location: center of chest
- Endocrine gland: thymus
- Color: Green
- Essential oils: rose, bergamot
- Crystal: rose quartz, emerald
- Deity: Maat, Esu
- Element: air
- Yoga pose: Maat Pose, Sphinx Pose, Cobra Pose
- Breath: Ujjayi pranayamas
- Meditation to the earth
- Journaling
- Imbalances: possessiveness, self-pity, clinginess, dispassion, meanness, feeling unworthy of love, holding back emotionally

Express Yourself

Vishuddha energy is located in the throat, the center of expression. This sound energy is referred to as the power of communication or energy of expression. Our ancient ancestors espoused right-speech in communication. According to ancient Kemetic wisdom, right speech is beautiful speech, which is God speech and divine speech. What comes out of our mouths are not simply words but speech as energy.

Blockage

We must be careful not to confuse talk or gossip with communication. We talk to and about our girlfriends but rarely do we communicate. We carry around so much unexpressed communication that it blocks this energy in our throats. To blurt out what's on our minds or tell it like it is does not reflect the power of expression.

Do you talk fast or have difficulty speaking your mind? Do you think your way is the right way? Are you arrogant and self-righteous? Do you hold your opinions or express inconsistent views? Do you feel a need to curse when conversing with others? Do you talk too much? Do you speak up for yourself? Do you listen? What does your voice sound like?

This chakra also informs our hearing and the ability to listen. How many times have you interrupted someone who is speaking? How many times have you wanted to say something so much that you stopped listening to the other person? Do people say things to you that you don't hear? When an elder is present, do you ask permission to speak?

What we learn as children determines our level of comfort with communication. For many of us, expressing ourselves was forbidden. We grew up with the adage, *Children should be seen not heard*. We heard phrases like "shut up," "don't talk back to me," and "I don't care what you have to say." At times, those phrases were paired with physical abuse. As a result, we were conditioned not to speak. Were you ever beaten or hit because you were talking or expressing yourself? Have you felt like something was stuck in your throat, preventing you from expressing yourself? What do you do when someone upsets you? Do you turn inward? Given our wariness about speaking, it's no wonder that many people have a difficult time expressing themselves. After a while, you may have become afraid to speak and attract people in your life, which reinforces your damaged throat energy. Your fear of either losing them or being unloved causes you to hide your truth.

Unlock the Energy

Unlock your throat energy. Shout if you have to, but release the energy. Tell someone that you love him or her. If someone has hurt you, release that as well. Unlearn what you have learned about expressing yourself. Learn to speak well and communicate from the heart. Engage in chanting, mantras, hekau, prayers, and music to encourage the healing of the throat chakra.

Perfect Journey

Legs-Up-the-Wall

Facing the wall, place the back of your pelvis against the wall and swing your legs up. Drop your sitting bones into the space next to the wall. (The sit bones are literally the bones under the flesh of your butt.) Open your arms out to the side. If your hamstrings feel tight, try turning your legs slightly in. Relax into the pose. Hold it for a minimum of five minutes.

Let go of any anxiety or tightness. Inhale a deep slow breath through your nose into your mouth, throat, tongue, ears, and neck. Exhale obstructions and constrictions in communication and expression. Place a turquoise on your throat chakra with the intent of clearing your inability to express yourself. Draw your breath into your throat chakra. Feel the energy of Tehuti, the god and lord of the divine word.

Neck Stretch

Sit in a comfortable position with your shoulders and back straight, arms loose by your sides. Loosen up your shoulders and neck muscles. Breathe normally. Lean your head backward, and inhale. Drop your head all the way forward without bending your body forward. Exhale as you lower your chin to your chest. Keep your shoulders relaxed. Repeat three times. Lift your head up and inhale. Exhale and loosen up. Feel your thyroid gland and digestive system healing, your nervous system calming down, and your fears and anxieties subsiding. Give yourself permission to speak. What do you want? What do you need? Speak your truth.

Neck Roll

Face forward and inhale deeply. Exhale as you drop your chin to your chest. Gently move your head in a circular motion from the left, inhaling until your head is tilted backward. Continue to roll your head in the same direction, exhaling until your chin is pressed into your chest again. Stretch gently before lifting your head, inhaling and exhaling. Inhale again, lower your head, exhale, and press your chin into your chest. Repeat the sequence in the opposite direction.

Throat Chakra

- Function: communication, speech, expression, listening, and hearing
- Location: Throat between the third and fifth vertebrae
- Endocrine gland: thyroid
- Color: deep blue
- Crystal: turquoise, sodalite, blue lace agate
- Essential oils: chamomile, sandalwood
- Deity: Tehuti
- Element: ether
- Yoga pose: Legs-up-the-wall, Neck Stretch, and Neck Roll
- Breath: breath awareness
- Meditation: On speaking truth
- Journaling
- Imbalances: anxiety, rudeness, braggadocio, isolation, chattiness, arrogance, unreliability, contradiction, opinionated

The Power of Knowing

Ajna, or the third eye, is located one millimeter above the eyebrows. It sits in the middle of forehead and connects you to your spiritual energy. Touch it with your index finger. This chakra energy is linked to the pineal gland, which is responsive to light. The pineal gland produces the hormone melatonin, which regulates sleep and waking up. Our third eye gives us insight so that we trust our inner guidance. It gives us access to intuition, knowing, inner perception, charisma, and detachment from material things. Awaken your energy of knowing.

Blockage

Blockage in this chakra manifests as self-righteousness, over-intellectualization, arrogance, underachievement, and a lack of discipline. In addition, we stop trusting our gut feelings

Unlock the Energy

What are you struggling with at this moment? Is there an issue in your life that shows you that you are indecisive? How do you make decisions? Some people resort to readings, others seek guidance; however, many of us make random decisions. Are you dealing with the reality of the situation or rationalizing it? How do you know whether you should marry that person, take that job, move, or divorce? What makes you decide to join a group or cut off your relationship with someone who was important to you? Do you ever get a feeling that you shouldn't do something and ignore it? What happens?

Most of the time, when we make a major decision, we do so without any insight or intuitive support. Only afterward do we talk about our feelings. If our descending chakras are not open, we cannot activate the third eye. To unlock this powerful energy, we must feel stable, secure, self-loving, transformative, unconditionally compassionate, and loving; otherwise, we might mistake arrogance and dogma for intuition and wisdom.

Perfect Journey

Stick Pose
Inhale. Sit on your mat, extend your legs straightforward from your hips. Exhale. Engage your pelvis in a neutral position. Inhale as you extend your spine upward and the palms of your hands press into the earth on both sides of near your sit bones.

Exhale. Engage the muscles of your leg, spread your toes, and press the tops of your femur bones downward.

Inhale. Push down and back into heels of your hands so that you feel your arms engage, your spine lengthen up, and your pelvis and chest ope.

Exhale slowly as you stretch your head away from your shoulders. Let your breath flow in and out as you draw your breath to your third eye, visualizing the deity—Horus, the soul eye. Focus your breath on the in-and-out movement. Then scan your body from head to toe and listen to each part of your body. As you breathe, visualize the color purple. Feel the vibration of the sapphire on the third eye.

Exhale negative thoughts. Inhale wisdom.

Eye Gazing

Let's practice eye gazing to improve concentration. Sit on a yoga mat in a comfortable cross-legged position. Feel relaxed and calm. Breathe normally.

Make a circle on a piece of paper. Hang it on a wall in front of you at the level of your eyes at a distance of about two meters away. Fix your gaze upon the sign.

Concentrate on the circle until your eyes start watering or feel the strain. Once this happens, close your eyes. Imagine that symbol to be between your eyebrows and concentrate upon that sign through the mind's eye. This increases the power of concentration and silence.

Brow Chakra

- Function: insight, intuitive thought, perception, knowledge, wisdom, charisma
- Location: above and between the eyebrows
- Endocrine gland: pineal
- Color: deep purple
- Crystal: sapphire, black opal
- Essential oils: sandalwood, amber
- Deity: Horus
- Element: light, thought
- Yoga pose: Meditation, Eye Gazing
- Breath: Alternate nostril breathing
- Meditation: stillness and silence
- Journaling
- Imbalances: spiritually disconnected, dogmatic, manipulative spiritual teachings, deceptive intelligence, authoritarian, undisciplined

The Hero

Spinal Twist

Beautiful Woman: Feel Good

Sahasrara, or the crown chakra, is the energy of pure consciousness, rebirth, and emancipation. Here lies the seat of divinity or awakening. It is our awakening that makes us beautiful, a goddess, or a queen, not Prada, Coach, false eyelashes, L'Oreal, hair texture or length, Remy, degrees, money, tight jeans, derrière size, sexual organs, tongue rings, lip rings, or tattoos. Only inner balance and the realization of the authentic self

Blockage

When this center is blocked, we live materialistically and egotistically. Our conversations are self-centered, egocentric, self-debasing, and limiting. We define ourselves by what we have and like, such as the make and model of the car we own and brand-name clothing we buy. We measure ourselves according to whom we've met or what we've achieved. We become preoccupied with external things. We become attached to our roles and positions until something happens to wake us up.

Other signs of blockage in the crown center are a sense of entitlement, egotism, and arrogance. There is a difference between confidence and egotism and self-respect and arrogance. Egotism and arrogance are unhealthy, whereas confidence and self-respect are healthy. Who we are is not what we say about ourselves, but what others experience. Egotism and arrogance encourages us to pretend to be someone else. However, pretending is no substitute for authenticity. Only when we stop bragging about ourselves do we become exceptional. If you want to embrace beauty, live with humility, consciousness, confidence, and self-respect.

Unlock the Energy

When spinning rhythmically, this center connects us to our true divine selves, not a caricature from television or a mistaken identity that has been handed down from history or unknowing caretakers. No longer do we have to pretend to be someone else. We become our divine selves-------- extraordinary.

We commit ourselves to school and to obtaining degrees. We travel to obtain certifications. We get our hair braided, which takes hours. We seek worldly treasures. However, all of these worldly successes and ego-gratifying measures pale in comparison to being whole, transform, enlighten and spiritual. Here, we remember who were, before the chaos, and become who we were meant to be--divine.

Enlightenment, self-actualization, self-realization, and peace exist. You are truly liberated and interconnected with all beings. You are no longer the great pretender. You have awakened.

Perfect Journey

Close your eyes. Release your frown, soften your face, and free your mind. Lie down on your back with your arms resting by your side. Gently face your palms up. Let gravity escort the weight of your head, shoulders, back, pelvis, and legs into the earth. Take a deep breath in and slowly exhale. Inhale a deep slow breath through your nose into your mouth, throat, tongue, ears, and neck. Let your breath flow in and out as you move your breath to your crown chakra. As you inhale deeply, feel the omnipresence of God, Allah, or the divine force Amun-Ra.

Allow the divine force to cascade through your body, releasing tension and enriching every cell with a divine consciousness that heals your thoughts from the past into the present.

Know that your life is perfect. Your financial situation, job, family, relationships, and health are life lessons. Feel the power within to transform your life. Let go of the mental chains that bond you to past realities. You are enlightened.

Allow your mind to rise above worldly issues and limitations. Begin to think of God., The Creator,, the Omnipotent Activate your divine energy as you embark on new experiences and an awakening. Experience silence. Visualize the color white or ultraviolent light. Through your breath, salute the divine energy within for 20 minutes. Enjoy *The Art of Feeling Good*.

Mummy Pose
Lie flat on your back. Close your eyes. Extend your legs two feet apart. Place your legs hip-width apart and let your feet fall open. Reach your arms down and out, shoulder-height with your arms one foot away from your body. Tuck your shoulder blades down while you roll your arms outward to leave your chest lifted and full. Make sure your palms face upward. Stretch your head away from your shoulders.

Take a few breaths with your mouth open to release the air held in the sinuses, mouth, and tracheal passageways. Continue with mouth breathing as long as you feel tense or fatigued. When you feel relaxation progressing over your mouth, gently close your mouth and breath with Ujjayi breath for some time.

Concentrate on your breath's wavelike motions. Then scan your body from head to feet, feeling and listening to each part's message in turn. Do you feel tense, nervous, or relaxed? After some time, encourage your thoughts to move more slowly.

Concentrate on the rising and subsiding energy in your body. Remain mentally alert yet physically passive for a minimum of 20 minutes. Surrender to the pull of gravity and your innate-relaxation reflex.

When you are finished, roll onto your right side, and curl up for a few moments of deep and slow breathing before you sit up in comfortable cross leg position.

Crown Chakra

- Function: spirit, divine wisdom, rebirth, and self-realization
- Location: top of the head, anterior fontanelle
- Endocrine gland: pituitary ("seat of the mind")
- Color: white, gold, violet
- Essential oils: lavender, valerian
- Crystals: Pearl, Amethyst, clear quartz
- Deity: God, Allah, Amun-Ra
- Element: pure spirit
- Yoga Pose: Mummy or Corpse
- Breath: breath awareness
- Meditation: guided on rebirth/contentment/infinite possibilities
- Journaling: write down your feelings, experiences, and insight
- Imbalances: worry, fatigue, indecisiveness, frustration, and psychosis

Appendix A

Yoga Poses

If practiced mindfully, yoga poses (asanas) can diminish and prevent diseases and facilitate balance and healing. In this section, I've identify the most commonly occurring diseases and associate them with a pose, breath, or meditation. With regular practice, symptoms should subside and balance will emerge. Please seek appropriate training before attempting these poses.

Stress
- Guided Meditation
- Alternate Nostril Breathing
- Mummy Pose
- Breath Awareness
- Sphinx Pose

Back Pain
- Forward Bend
- Fish Pose
- Cobra Pose
- Locust
- Cat Pose
- Spinal Twist

- Alternate Nostril Breathing
- Meditation and Relaxation
- Downward facing Dog

Constipation
- Forward-folding Bending Pose
- Pelvic Tilt and Thrust
- Sphinx Pose
- Spinal Twist
- Breath of Liberation

Menstrual Problems
- Pelvic Tilt and Thrust
- Forward Bends

Heart Disease
- Corpse Pose
- Alternate Nostril Breathing
- Yoga Nidra

Hypertension
- Corpse Pose
- Pranic Breathing
- Reclining Bound Angle Pose
- Mummy Pose
- Breath of Liberation

Digestive Disorders
- Spinal Twist
- Forward Bend

Diabetes
- Bow Pose
- Spinal Twist
- Ujjayi Breathing
- Meditation and Relaxation

Headaches
- Neck Roll
- The Mummy Pose
- Meditation

Insomnia
- Neck and Shoulder Stretches

Anxiety
- Shoulder Stand
- The Corpse
- Alternate Nostril Breathing

Depression
- Bridge Pose
- Half-Headstand
- Dog Pose
- Àse Yoga Freestyle Flow

Panic Attacks
- Shoulder Stand
- The Corpse
- Ujjayi
- Alternate Nostril Breathing

Appendix B

Self-Healing Oath

An affirmation is a saying that we repeat because we want to call it into existence in our lives. The following spiritual affirmations seek to raise our consciousness and transform our lives:

1. I will strive to achieve self-knowledge.
2. I will no longer base my worth on things.
3. I will open my heart, unconditionally.
4. I will love myself.
5. I will become connected with my energy centers to create a whole self.
6. I will take care of my body, mind, and spirit.
7. I will accept responsibility for my actions.
8. I will eat natural and whole foods.
9. I will balance my eating, sleeping, consuming, and sensory stimulation.
10. I will forgive others and myself.
11. I will meditate on a daily basis.
12. I will acknowledge my ancestors on daily basis.
13. I will read.
14. I will eat a home-cooked meal 90 percent of the time.
15. I will engage in self-study

16. I will declutter my life.
17. I will practice yoga.
18. I will let go of anger against anyone, past or present.
19. I will follow the rules of Maat, the eight limbs of yoga.
20. I will respect myself.

_____ Name
_____ Date

Bibliography

AHRQ: 2008 National Healthcare Disparities and Quality Reports." Agency for Healthcare Research and Quality (AHRQ) Home. http://www.ahrq.gov/qual/qrdr08.htm

"African American Women and Depression FACT SHEET. " National Alliance on Mental Illness, 2009. Retrieved from http://nami.org

Arewa, Caroline Shola. Opening to Spirit: Contacting the Healing Power of the Chakras& Honoring African Spirituality. London: Thorsons, 1998.

Armah, Ayi Kwei. Two Thousand Seasons. London: Heinemann, 1973.

Ashby, Muata, and Ashby Karen Asha. Initiation into Egyptian Yoga: The Secrets of Sheti. Miami, Fla.: Cruzian Mystic Books, 1996.

Ashby, Muata, and Ashby Karen Vijaya. Egyptian Yoga: Movements of the Gods and Goddesses. Miami, Fla.: Cruzian Mystic Books, 2001.

Britt, Alice B. "African-Americans Substance Abuse and Spirituality." www. minoritynurse.com/substance-abuse/african-americans-substance-abuse-and-spirituality.

Browder, Anthony T. From the Browder file: 22 essays on the African American experience. Washington, D.C.: Institute of Karmic Guidance, 1989.

Bynum, Edward. The African Unconscious. New York: Teachers College Press, 1999.

"Chemical Relaxers, Fibroids and Black Women: How it All Started. The Urban Scientist, Scientific American Blog Network." Scientific American Blog Network. http://blogs.scientificamerican.com/urban-scientist/2012/03/07/chemical-relaxers-fibroids-and-black-women-how-it-all-started/

Crupi, Anthony. BET: Population, Spending Skyrocketing for African Americans. Ad week, Breaking News in Advertising, Media and Technology. http://www.adweek.com/news/advertising-branding/bet-population-spending-skyrocketing-african-americans-114661

"Fibroids." Philadelphia Black Women's Health Alliance. http://www.blackwomenshealthproject.org/aafibroids.htm.

"How Yoga can Treat Serious Medical Conditions." http://Oprah.com/health

Jacq, Christian. The Wisdom of Ptah-Hotep: Spiritual Treasures From the Age Of The Pyramids. London: Constable & Robinson Ltd., 2006.

Kamalu, Chukwunyere. Foundations of African thought: A Worldview Grounded In The African Heritage of

Religion, Philosophy, Science, and Art. London: Karnak House, 1990.

Kiau, Kimbwandelende Kia Bunseki. Self-Healing Power and Therapy: Old Teachings From Africa. New York: Vantage Press, 1991.

Lester, Julius, & Tom Feelings. To Be A Slave. New York: Dial Press, 1968.

"Lives of Women of Color Create Risk for Depression." Women's eNews." Women's eNews. www.womensenews. org/story/mental-health/011001/lives-women-color-create-risk-depression.

Mitchell, Stephen. Bhagavad Gita: A New Translation. New York: Three Rivers Press, 2000.

Pfeffer, Rachel. In Post Racial America Prisons Feast on Black Girls. Mar 15, 2011. www.ethnoblog.newamericamedia. org/2011/03/in-post-racial-america-prisons-   feast-on-black-girls-1.php.

Rouse, Deborah L. RESPECT BLACK: February 2012. http:// respectblack.blogspot.com/2012_02_01_archive.html

Sertima, Ivan. Black Women In Antiquity. New Brunswick [N.J.] U.S.A.: Transaction Books, 1984.

Singleton, Mark. Yoga Body: The Origins Of Modern Posture Practice. Oxford: Oxford University Press, 2010.

Source: Procter & Gamble Co., P&G/Essence poll. "Marketing to Women's Conference." www.m2w.biz/fast_facts.php. www.m2w.biz/fast_facts.php

Stolberg, Sheryl Gay. "Beautiful, Also, Are The Souls Of My Black Sisters. www. kathmanduk2.wordpress.com.

"Statistics on Lupus." Lupus Foundation Of America. www.lupus.org/webmodules/webarticlesnet_ newsroomreporters

White, Deborah G.. Ain't I a woman? Female Slaves In The Antebellum South. revised edition. W.W. Norton & Company, Inc, 1979.

Wilson, Allan. "Mitochondrial DNA and Human Evolution." Nature. no. 325 (1985): 31-36. www.nature.com/nature/ journal/v325/n6099/abs/325031a0.html (accessed

Zangrando, Robert. "About Lynching." Excerpted from a longer article in *The Reader's Companion to American History*. Ed. Eric Foner and John A. Garraty. Houghton Mifflin Co1991.

I have come to be a protector unto thee. I waft unto thee air for thy nostrils, and the north wind which cometh forth from the god Tem unto thy nose. I have made whole for thee thy windpipe. I make thee to live like a god. Thine enemies have fallen under thy feet. I have made thy word to be true before Nut, and thou art mighty before the gods.
—Aset